CC WICKRAMARATNE

WITH **DISHAN WICKRAMARATNE** & **HAL DONALDSON**

MY ADVENTURE IN FAITH

How one man dared to trust God for the impossible

FOREWORDS BY
DAVID YONGGI CHO & **RICK WARREN**

FOREWORDS BY **DAVID YONGGI CHO**
AND **RICK WARREN**

MY ADVENTURE IN FAITH

BY COLTON WICKRAMARATNE

WITH **DISHAN WICKRAMARATNE**
AND **HAL DONALDSON**

My Adventure in Faith
How one man dared to trust God for the impossible
By Colton Wickramaratne with Dishan Wickramaratne
and Hal Donaldson

Printed in the United States of America
ISBN: 1-880689-17-0
Copyright 2007, Onward Books, Inc., Dishan
Wickramaratne

Cover design by KeyArt

Scripture quotations are from the *King James Version* of
the Bible unless otherwise noted. Scripture quotations
marked *NKJV* are taken from the *New King James
Version*. Copyright 1979, 1980, 1982, Thomas Nelson,
Inc. Publishers. Scripture quotations marked *NIV* are
taken from the *New International Version*. Copyright
1973, 1978, 1984, International Bible Society.

DEDICATION

Dedicated to Susanne, my wife of more than 50 years. My adventure in faith would have been a daunting—if not impossible—task without her wholehearted commitment to the Lord and our marriage. Through the years she demonstrated unflinching faith and a willingness to make sacrifices and endure hardship in order to follow the leading of the Lord. In times of crisis she displayed a quiet assurance and offered untold wisdom and insight. Tirelessly she served our family and many others in the community. I am eternally thankful that God gave me a companion who could trust our Creator for the impossible.

CONTENTS

God has a plan and a purpose for your life. Heb 11:6

Pastor Colton.

Wickramaratne

FOREWORDS

I would like to commend the autobiography entitled, *My Adventure in Faith*, written by Colton Wickramaratne along with Dishan Wickramaratne and Hal Donaldson. It is a chronicle of the true life experiences of a great man of God.

In this exciting and edifying book you will find Colton Wickramaratne preaching the gospel message in stadiums throughout Asia, Africa, and Latin America. You will be thrilled by the 55 chapters that bring his unique and noble life into focus.

You will find the faith that led one of our most beloved and honored men of God from glory to glory throughout his life. You will discover the true meaning of love, faith, and hope in following the Lord Jesus.

Colton Wickramaratne has left a legacy that his son Dishan and countless men and women should try to emulate, all to the glory of the Lord Jesus Christ.

David Yonggi Cho
Chairman
Church Growth International

My Adventure in Faith is the story of how God can use an ordinary man in extraordinary ways. It shows how someone committed to God's purposes can be used by God to bring others into God's family. Colton Wickramaratne's story will encourage you to live out your faith in practical ways—just as it already has helped millions of people around the world to do more than just listen to God's Word. They have become "doers of his word"—active participants in God's initiatives.

Colton's life is devoted to communicating the gospel of Jesus Christ and to encouraging other believers to share their faith. His "adventure in faith" provides a practical model for young Christian leaders who understand "it's not about you," ones who are prepared for the exciting journey that comes from a purpose-driven life. Colton founded the People's Church in Colombo, Sri Lanka. His son Dishan now leads this purpose-driven congregation.

As you read *My Adventure in Faith*, you will see that faith is not content to look at our human limitations. It will catapult you into a place of trusting God—so you may fulfill His purpose for your life.

> Rick Warren
> Pastor, Saddleback Church
> Author, *Purpose Driven Life*

ACKNOWLEDGMENTS

I wish to express my sincere appreciation to many friends who have invested in my life and this book project, including:

My godly parents and family: My father and mother prayed me through to salvation. They were my first pastors.

William and Alvera Farrand, Vincent Abrahams, Arthur Speldewinde and Geoffrey Beling—who had a great influence on my life and ministry.

Mark and Huldah Buntain, Clarence and Irene Cope, Murray and Ellen McLees, Syvelle and Lovie Phillips, Ronald and Rosalyn Prinzing, Roy and Odelle Sapp, and Oliver Summers—who believed in me and became partners in my vision.

Florence Pokorney—who heard from God and supported me through Bible school.

Carl and Bertha Graves, Harold and Beatrice Kohl, Rosa Reineker and all the missionaries and pastors God used to enlarge my faith.

Elphege and Ila Fernando, Ronald and Rita Jesudason, Jacob and AnnaGreta Perera, Linton and Birdie

Dassenaike, my eldest brother Andrew, and my sister Anita—who stood with us from the early years to make our vision a reality.

Paul Beling, David Beling and Gerald Senn for their unstinting support during the formative years of the church.

All the pastors, elders, deacons, Timotheans, lay leaders, office staff, church members and friends of People's Church Colombo—who stood with me and Susanne to accomplish God's plan.

Our three sons—Chrysantha, Eran and Dishan—who walked the rugged path with us and now with their wives—Menaka, Kushlani and Jayani—carry on the work.

Our daughter, Roshani—the gift God gave us to brighten our latter years along with our grandchildren—Dhishan, Sohanya, Sasha, Shyara, Rajeev and Dilani.

David and June Beling, Paul Beling, Ila Fernando, Marie De Silva and Anne Vanden Driesen for the assistance given in preparing this book.

Hal Donaldson and my son Dishan, for assisting me in telling my story.

ENDORSEMENTS

In a world where profits matter, the motivation for selling a book is often driven by the desire to achieve high readership for the purpose of financial gains. This book is different. It aims to touch lives through a personal account of a life wholly committed to a cause that money can never buy. Colton Wickramaratne lives life with a "never-say-die" zeal and commitment. He has inspired my life for the last 35 years and I know this book will do the same for you.

> Dr. Robert Lim, Founding Chairman,
> JECPP (300 churches in the Philippines)
> Founding Pastor,
> Evangel Family Church, Singapore

For a long time I felt that we must have the story of this giant of the Asian church in print so that a wider audience would be inspired and challenged to "expect great things from God and attempt great things for God," as William Carey said. So I was delighted when I was asked to write a blurb for Pastor Colton's autobiography. I expected to be inspired by reading this book and that happened. But I did not expect God to speak to me as clearly as He did through this reading. You too will be inspired and spoken to by reading not so much about Pastor Colton as about the wonderful God he has so faithfully served.

Dr. Ajith Fernando, National Director,
Youth for Christ, Sri Lanka
Author and Bible teacher

It has been my privilege for many years to follow the life of Colton Wickramaratne. I have sat on boards with him and fellowshipped and communed with him in many ways along life's pathway. Throughout many, many years of relationship, my appreciation and respect for him have grown every day. This book, *My Adventure in Faith*, is just a small insight to the great exploits God has done through this great servant of the Lord. I believe it will be an inspiration and blessing to thousands who have not had the privilege of knowing him personally, but who can get a glimpse into his life through the pages of this work. I give my sincere recommendation to all readers to get a little taste of the life of one of the greatest servants of the Lord on the face of the earth.

Dr. L. John Bueno, Executive Director
Assemblies of God World Missions

I have known Dr. Colton Wickramaratne for many years and have heard him tell his adventure in faith under the rich anointing that has resulted in many believing and accepting Jesus Christ as Lord and Savior. I also know of many who were backslidden and returned to the Lord as well as others who were healed, delivered and called to the ministry.

This book will be a blessing to all those who are serving the Lord. It will rekindle the fire of the Holy Spirit in you and bring a fresh vision to make us worthy servants before Jesus returns. I am so glad he put his adventure in faith in writing.

Dr. Prince Guneratnam, Senior Pastor
Calvary Church, Kuala Lumpur, Malaysia
General Superintendent Emeritus
Assemblies of God of Malaysia
Vice Chairman, World Assemblies of God
Fellowship

Rev. Colton Wickramaratne's autobiographical book is powerful and yet practical. It will be an indispensable book to all young leaders around the world to grow in faith. It could change an ordinary person to an extraordinary one for Christ. His life of faith has been a great inspiration to me personally to build a great church in Chennai, India. He has invested his life for the younger generation and he has many Timothys as his spiritual sons. It is a book you will read and use often; it will change your faith life.

Rev. David Mohan
All India General Superintendent,
Assemblies of God
Senior Pastor, New Life Assembly of God,
Chennai, India

The time for this book is long overdue! Rev. Colton is a mighty apostle and prophet in our time. My wife and I have both been touched by his ministry since we were children. From the very first year of our ministry we have been involved with Rev. Colton and the People's Church, having ministered there many times. He has been an apostle to our church from the very first year it began and we have seen him minister with signs and wonders throughout the years. We have been in their home many times, having lived with them for two and a half months at one time. We can without hesitation say that he is one of the humblest ministers, completely down to earth, living very simply, investing everything into the Kingdom. His life has had a major impact on us and our ministry. I know this book will undoubtedly have an impact on your life.

> Rev. Rick Seaward
> Founding Pastor, Victory Family Centre,
> Singapore

I consider it a great privilege to write a few lines concerning *My Adventure in Faith*. Colton Wickramaratne is a great man of God and a living saint. God has given me the privilege of knowing him and his family very personally and also to be with him in his outreach meetings. Indeed, God has used him in a supernatural way. His very life is saturated with instances of divine intervention. It is God who has led him step by step by His eternal hand. I am thankful to God for speaking to His great apostle to put the whole thing in writing, so that posterity will know that "walking with God" can be a reality, even in this 21st century. It will be a great encouragement, especially, to all who wish to do God's ministry with power. The life of Dr. Wickramaratne could be summarized in the following verse given by the Lord as a testimony for David's life:

". . . He raised up for them David as king, to whom also He gave testimony and said, 'I have found David the son of Jesse, a man after My own heart, who will do all My will'" (Acts 13:22, NKJV).

I am sure the life of every reader of this great book shall also be transformed likewise.

Dr. D.G.S. Dhinakaran
Founder, Jesus Calls Ministries

INTRODUCTION

Every son who is blessed with a caring father wants to believe his father will live forever. You tend to project an air of immortality around a man who unselfishly loves you and faithfully shapes your life into your adult years—a man who offers wisdom at every critical point of decision—a man who stands as a tower of strength and encouragement when life threatens to steamroll you. I have such a father.

My father, Colton Wickramaratne, tirelessly gives of himself for his family, his church, his nation, and even his world. He may stand just a few inches over 5 feet, but he is a giant by any measure in the kingdom of God. His legacy as a leader is remarkable: pastoring village churches, leading a vibrant congregation in our capital city, overseeing our national fellowship, coordinating international leadership congresses, and more.

My father has lived in the arena of faith. He has shown me that faith is not content to look at today and the limitations of human experience. Faith catapults us into the realm of the Spirit. Faith promises us a life beyond this one, a life undeterred by this world's sorrows and blessed with undiluted, eternal fellowship with our Heavenly Father.

My earthly father's relationship with our Heavenly Father has made all the difference in his life, and in mine. His passion to communicate the gospel of Jesus Christ is boundless. He exudes an energy of the Holy Spirit that seems ready to burst forth at any moment.

I have seen my father convey that divine conviction to thousands of people in Asia, Africa, North America and Latin America. I have watched the same vibrant truth being offered in intimate simplicity to a lonely and hurting man, woman or child during a "chance" encounter. However, my father will be quick to tell you that in God's economy there really are only divinely appointed encounters.

Colton Wickramaratne has two ambitions. He is always looking for the next opportunity given by the Holy Spirit to share God's message of eternal life with lost souls. And he is always seeking to multiply the gospel proclamation by awakening a similar passion for souls in others. He tirelessly strives to expand the ministry of countless men and women, knowing that the influence he helps to garner for fellow servants of Christ will ultimately result in more glory to Christ himself.

This book allows both of my father's life ambitions to find expression. It speaks plainly of the gospel, or "good news," of Jesus Christ to any reader who has yet to discover the joy of knowing the Savior; and these chapters offer a mandate to another generation of men and women called to share that gospel, inspiring readers to give their all for the greatest cause in eternity.

For years I have encouraged my father to publish an account of his life and ministry. I am grateful that he has now done so with the conviction that this is God's time to tell this story. This is not a narrative whitewashed of life's struggles and mistakes. Colton Wickramaratne did not suddenly emerge as a statesman of the church whom I love and honor today. Despite his upbringing in a Christian home, he once lived in open opposition to the gospel. He shares some of his experiences from those dark years in the pages that follow. And he is just as honest about the years of spiritual growth God brought about in his life once he made the vital decision to follow Christ. It was growth marked by growing pains.

No one should confuse this book for hagiography; it is a starkly honest autobiography. It is this honesty that makes this book a must-read for every person who is on a similar journey of faith. My faith has grown by watching my father, as well as my mother, live out the gospel, face up to personal failure, and press forward to even greater levels of spiritual victory.

My prayer is that *My Adventure in Faith* will not simply be read as another autobiography of a man's struggles and triumphs in ministry. I pray that it becomes a personal journal, in a sense, for countless men and women whom God will choose to further His purposes and expand His kingdom throughout a lost and dying world. I pray that *My Adventure in Faith* will inspire your own faith adventure.

Dishan Wickramaratne

A PERSONAL NOTE

The Secret of the Success of My Life and Ministry

To all who read this book, this will become the most important chapter.

My wife is the key to my life and ministry. "Whoso findeth a wife findeth a good thing" (Proverbs 18:22). "A wife of noble character who can find? She is worth far more than rubies. Her husband has full confidence in her and lacks nothing of value. She brings him good, not harm, all the days of her life" (Proverbs 31:10-12, NIV).

My life, my vision and ministry could have been destroyed many times. I could have lost everything; you would never have read this book if not for my wife and her vital role in this entire episode.

My wife was like my guardian angel for my protection. She was sensitive to the moving of the Holy Spirit, she detected the dangers and began to intercede in great anguish. She went through much suffering which I did not understand. Therefore I did not treasure her sacrificial labor of love as I should have. She was a God-given life partner to me. She was a faithful wife, a loving mother, a strong, wise partner in my life and ministry. When I had the vision in 1957, I woke her on that day and said how God met me.

She said, "Tell me."

I said, "I made a commitment to God and you must make a commitment to me."

She said, "Your God is my God; your people are my

people; where you go, I will go and stand together with you." This commitment has been kept all these years.

Once a friend of ours, the Reverend Syvelle Phillips, told Susanne it is very difficult to live with a prophet. This was true, but I thank God for her who had much grace and understanding to walk together with me.

I praise God for her, and my advice to you is value your partner and work together and you will be blessed of the Lord.

MY ADVENTURE IN FAITH

YOUNG COLTON, ANNA LEWINI, SAM AND LILLIAN
WICKRAMARATNE WITH BELIEVERS IN MAKEVITA.

Encounter with the Spirit

1919. Colombo, Sri Lanka, was hot, humid and bustling as passengers exited the oceanliner and made a valiant attempt to reconnect with their luggage. A Scandinavian woman, her blond hair gathered beneath a Parisian hat, stood out among the copper-skinned dockworkers and young Sri Lankan women wearing bright-colored saris. The woman, Anna Lewini, was a promising Danish actress on her way to India to make a film. Her ship had stopped for a brief respite in Sri Lanka.

During her stay, Anna held revival meetings at Colombo's Tower Hall. She believed in the power of the Holy Spirit and was part of a growing worldwide Pentecostal phenomenon. My father, Sam, a customs officer and Baptist lay preacher, attended Anna's meetings along with my mother. When Anna prayed for my parents, they both received the baptism in the Holy Spirit, as evidenced by speaking in tongues.

My father's encounter with the Spirit of God put him at odds with fellow Christians who had not shared his experience. But this did not stop my father. He was a man who, when God wanted him to do something, didn't turn back. He sensed a call to be a full-time minister and asked God to make that possible.

When my father and mother were married, the dowry system was still prevalent in Sri Lanka, then known as Ceylon. Since the husband would care for the wife for the rest of her life, it was expected that the wife would enter the marriage with a substantial contribution. My mother's parents had contributed a sizeable dowry, yet my father was forced to use the money to support the family as he ministered without a salary.

Excluded from the church he once attended because of his stance on the Holy Spirit, my father looked for every opportunity to preach a full gospel that clearly connected the Spirit's powerful ministry with every aspect of the believer's life.

But without the support of a church and the dowry funds exhausted, living became difficult. Often, they did not know how they would get through the week.

"Let's pray about it," was their simple expectation of faith.

God often provided the money they needed through persons they had never met. They learned to expect miracles. They learned to believe in the power and providence of God.

Despite hardship and ridicule, my father and mother were among those used of God to start the Pentecostal work in Sri Lanka. Even before I was born, my parents had established a foundation of uncompromising faith equal to every hardship they would face. Little did I know that faith would become bedrock in my own life and allow me to overcome the onslaughts of the enemy. Satan knew the work God had called me to accomplish, so he went to great lengths to destroy my life and ministry. He stalked my soul. But, like my parents, it was my faith in the power and protection of God that would allow me to fulfill the destiny God had placed on my life.

Mother's Miracle

My parents had nine children—seven boys and two girls. But on November 2, 1931, I almost died at birth.

At that time in Sri Lanka, the doctor or midwife would come to the home and assist the mother. I was told that at the time of my birth my mother's labor pains—even with the midwife's care—seemed to go on forever. When complications developed my father summoned a doctor.

"Mr. Wickramaratne," he told my father, "your wife cannot have this baby at home. You must take her immediately to the hospital."

My impoverished father did not hesitate, despite not having the money to pay for medical services. He knew my mother's life hung in the balance. She was rushed to an operating room where other doctors examined her.

Father paced the hall, waiting for news. His shirt collar clung to his neck and sweat stung his eyes. This was a hospital in the tropics, after all, and long before the era of climate control. Open windows begrudgingly admitted a humid sea breeze and the noise of bustling city dwellers, unaware of the life-and-death struggles within these walls.

The click of a latch echoed through the hall. The doctors filed out of the operating room and grimly approached my father.

"Your wife is in a serious condition," the physician said. "Whom do you want?"

"'Whom do I want?'" my father asked, confused and fearful at the same time.

There was an awkward pause. "Do you want to save your wife or your baby? We cannot save them both."

My father paused. "Save my wife," he said, choking back the tears. He knew my chances of survival were slim but he hoped the doctors could at least pull my mother through.

In the operating room, Mother struggled with the pain of frustrated childbirth. She knew her spasms of agony were no ordinary labor pains. All seemed lost. Yet, she had great faith within her tiny frame. She gathered her hands together and prayed. She didn't care who was listening. "Lord," she cried out, "You have always done the impossible for us. Lord, You can save me *and* this baby. You can do a miracle."

Mother was not content to plead her case before the throne of heaven with one quick prayer. She began to fervently worship the Lord from her hospital bed, completely trusting that her miracle—and my miracle—was on the way.

The medical team stood by assuming they would be forced to operate.

Yet Mother continued to worship, her hands raised. Her prayers touched heaven and left every problem of earth behind.

Doctors and nurses stood paralyzed at the spectacle of a praying woman in the throes of birth pangs. But while Mother was worshipping, another lady was rushed into the operating room. She was writhing in pain. All attention shifted to this woman. The doctors left my mother's side for a moment.

Meanwhile, Mother's own side of the operating room seemed to hover in blissful isolation. Not a single menacing scalpel pointed in her direction.

Little did the physicians know that in that moment a

divine Doctor stepped into the operating room. No human eye saw His tender hands begin to care for the needs of my mother and me. Suddenly, contractions began to move steadily across my mother's body. She seemed to push and relax in perfect harmony with the unheard coaxing of a heavenly voice. Without the assistance of a single doctor, nurse or midwife, without the application of a single medical instrument, I was born—a 9-pound miracle.

My mother always believed God had spared my life for a reason. She believed He had a work for me to accomplish. So, even when I turned my back on God as a youth, she never lost hope. Somehow she knew God still had a purpose for my life.

MY ADVENTURE IN FAITH

YOUNG COLTON DURING HIS BIBLE SCHOOL DAYS.

Ungrateful Rebel

Life constantly mixes joy and pain. The pure joy God intends for us will not be fully experienced until we are with Him for eternity. Here and now, even moments of profound happiness can be marred by unexpected tragedy. Such was the case with my birth. During the very hours my mother and I survived our ordeal at the hospital, one of my sisters was losing her battle with a serious illness.

To this day, the proximity of my miracle and her death is a mystery. For superstitious families in our community, however, I was an evil child. My arrival, they said, brought about my sister's death. But Father and Mother, even in their sorrow, knew that God's purposes for my sister were just as wonderful as His purposes for me. My sister, through God's boundless gift of grace, had been ushered into His presence to live forever outside the reach of illness, pain or any variety of sorrow.

My parents' unwavering faith in God's love and goodness permeated our family life. Every morning when we awoke, we gave time to prayer and Bible reading—without that, there was no breakfast. By lunchtime on Saturday, while other children had already spent half a day playing or going about chores, we had spent the morning in family prayer and Scripture memorization. Every evening Father led a family prayer meeting. All of this was intended to give us the necessary tools for living a godly life, but resentment and rebellion were growing within me.

When I was 17, Father established a church outside Colombo in the village of Makevita. The people who attended thought I was a respectable minister's son, but I was moving farther from God each day.

I plotted my escape from the church and my confining lifestyle. I convinced my Sunday school teacher, a devout Christian woman, to start a poultry business.

"We'll raise some hens and I'll sell their eggs for you," I said. She readily agreed to buy the hens.

In no time I was making regular trips to Colombo with dozens of eggs to sell. But I collected the money and stashed it away for myself. I would simply tell the woman the customers promised to pay later.

In the city, however, I found opportunities to satisfy my sinful desires and a way to leave behind all the family prayer meetings and Bible studies I had come to despise.

One day I gathered my clothes and slipped away to the city—planning never to return. I made my rounds to collect the money for the eggs and kept it for myself. Ahead of me appeared to be the limitless possibilities of life in the great city without my family obligations.

"I don't want to be compelled to be a Christian," I would tell my city friends as we pursued days of self-indulgence. "I don't want to be brainwashed."

Some weeks after I ran away, my parents sent my two older brothers, Andrew and Calvin, to find me and escort me home. I was always small for my age, but I had a violent temper. I had suspected that Mother and Father might attempt to force my return, and I had primed my emotions to put up whatever fight was necessary. The day my brothers found me, however, I knew from their faces that I would come out the loser in any scrap I started. So I meekly accompanied them to the train station. They held me like a couple of police officers. Their stern demeanor led the people around us to believe I was a juvenile delinquent in custody.

On the train I sat between them. My arms soon ached from the force of their grip. There was a series of jolts as the engine heaved against the line of cars with bursts of steam. Soon we were leaving Colombo behind and with it all my dreams of independence. My dread of returning home was augmented by the realization that my father would surely give me the thrashing of my life. As far as I was concerned, I should have the freedom to do what I wanted regardless of my family's wishes. I was the center of my universe.

The train came to a station and braked to allow dozens of passengers to board the already crowded compartments. After a whistle and another burst of steam, the train was moving again. But I had a plan.

"I need to visit the toilet," I said to Andrew.

At first he didn't believe me. "Quiet," he muttered as he reasserted his grip on my arm.

"Please," I begged.

"All right," Andrew muttered. "But if I have to come look for you, you'll regret it."

"Of course," I said. "I understand."

The moment they released me, I bolted for freedom. I heard them yell behind me, but I was small enough to squeeze between standing passengers. In seconds I reached the end of the compartment, opened the door and jumped. Fortunately I landed and rolled through tall grass, just avoiding the rushing steel wheels. Bruised and covered in cuts, a smile crossed my face as I looked up to see my brothers shaking their fists at me through an open window.

"This time you'll never catch me," I yelled. "You'll never see me again."

Knocking at Death's Door

During the hours it took to walk back to Colombo, I hoped my family would simply give up on forcing me to come home. But it didn't occur to me that my tiny nest egg of stolen money wouldn't last forever. I soon was exhausting my resources and, like the scriptural prodigal son, I found myself impoverished, practically friendless and completely in despair.

Why was I born? my tormented mind would ask as my empty stomach grumbled ever more loudly. *What am I doing? Where will I go?* I couldn't answer any of the questions. *There's no meaning to life,* I decided.

At the end of my rope, I turned to the only friend I had left and asked him to get me a bottle of rat poison, as his father was a pharmacist.

"This is nasty stuff," my friend said.

"The rats have been horrible since the last rains," I responded.

My bluff worked. Poison and coins exchanged hands.

I went back to the tiny room I could no longer afford, and wrote three letters. In one I thanked my parents for all they had done for me; then I told them I was disgusted with life and so I was ending it. A letter to the police department assured them there was no foul play and I was taking my life voluntarily. The third letter was to a close girlfriend of mine. I knew my death would cause her a good deal of sorrow. I wanted her to rest easy knowing this was for the best and it was entirely my choice.

I took these letters and went to a deserted botanical garden in Gampaha, not far from Colombo. I sat under a giant coconut tree close to a stream. It was a beautiful sunny afternoon, one that seemed to mock the clouds of turmoil in my heart. I sat there and put the three letters under a stone. I leaned against the tree and contemplated using the bottle of poison.

"I know there is no God," I said to the sky. "That's why I can't answer all the questions I have. What's the use of living?"

I took the bottle of poison and pulled out the cork. I knew the poison was probably quite caustic, and I feared that my mouth would burn. So I held the bottle above my gaping mouth with the intent of pouring it straight down my throat. I wavered, then let loose one final volley at God.

"God, somehow I know You are not there. But, if You *are* there, I don't want to meet You somewhere and have You say that I never gave You a chance. If You are there, I'm telling You . . . meet me now."

Instantly my anger gave way to desperation. Tears surfaced and I began to pray. "I have nothing to offer You," I said in a broken voice. "But I will offer my life to You if . . ."

Then the clouds of doubt began to close in again. "But if You are not there," I shouted, "it's perfectly all right with me because I *know* that You aren't there."

Finding new courage, I took the bottle and lifted it to pour the poison right into my throat.

And that's when I saw it: tacked to the very tree I was under was an enormous poster. To this day, I cannot tell you who would have gone into that neglected botanical garden to put up a poster no one was likely to see. But I know it was divinely placed in order to prevent my plummet into eternity.

I quickly held back the poison and turned around to read the poster. It looked like it had been written to me personally.

"If you are discouraged, if you are disheartened, if you have come to the end of life's journey and you don't know what to do, remember Jesus Christ is the answer to all of your problems. Come this evening to the central YMCA at 6 o'clock."

I shoved the bottle into my pocket, saying, "Okay, I will go, find out what they're saying, and disrupt the meeting if it's just a lot of nonsense. They'll regret putting up that poster in the middle of nowhere."

MY
ADVENTURE
IN FAITH

COLTON, SUSANNE WITH JACOB PERERA, LYNN JANZ AND
GEOFFREY BELING AT IMPETUS '80.

CHAPTER 5

Moment of Decision

God had arrested my attention and spared my life from the poison. Yet, I began to grumble and doubt whether attending the meeting was worth my time: "I'm sure this is another gimmick of some foreigner, maybe an American who has come to deceive our people by putting the fear of God and hell into them, and bring in some Western religion."

Nevertheless, with the bottle of poison and suicide letters jammed into my pocket, I set out for Colombo and the YMCA auditorium. Along the way, I stopped at a pub to get some alcohol to fortify my courage and remove my inhibitions.

After a few drinks, I was determined to vent all my frustration on those religious fanatics. I would create a real scene and make it clear to all who gathered that Christianity was just another form of brainwashing. If they called the police, so what? I had kept the poison. I would just drink it quickly and put myself out of my misery.

The room was crowded with youth and they were listening intently to a visiting American evangelist from Youth for Christ. If I had possessed any spiritual sense, I would have felt the electricity in the air. God was dealing powerfully with young men and women across the auditorium, calling them to a life of faith and sacrifice. But I was a different story. I was defiant and courting death.

Depressed, suicidal and inebriated, I sat in the last row and camouflaged my inner feelings with an outer display of bravado. I didn't listen to what the evangelist was saying. Instead, childishly, I began to throw paper balls and cough loudly and clear my throat in the most disgusting manner. There were some young girls sitting in front of me. I began to pull their braided hair and make an even-greater nuisance of myself.

Toward the end of the message it was as if God suddenly amplified my hearing and my attention was arrested beyond my control. I heard these words very clearly: "If you have come to the end of life's journey, remember, Jesus Christ is the answer. He will meet your need if you will just come to Him."

Before I realized it, I was walking to the front of the auditorium. The platform was high and the preacher was pacing back and forth with his interpreters, pleading for young people to make the one decision that would transform their lives for all eternity.

As he came near the edge of the platform, I reached up to grab his pants leg. "Preacher," I yelled up to him, my small fist in a death-grip around a wad of fabric, "I don't believe you."

Public speakers react to disturbances such as this in different ways. Some post bodyguards to block entrances to the platform. Others motion for altar workers to escort the person away. But this preacher was unfazed. "Just a minute, young man," he said through the interpreter, calmly extricating his leg. "I have not finished with my altar call." He continued urging the young crowd to give their lives to Jesus.

Many youth responded. Then he turned to his father, a magnificent Christian elder who was traveling with him, and said, "Father, could you help this young man?"

That dear old man didn't hesitate a moment. He came down from the platform and put his arms around me. For an instant I welcomed the embrace, but then my fears resurfaced. I threw down his arms. I was suddenly suspicious of him; I was afraid his intent was to hypnotize me or put me into a trance. "Don't touch me," I said angrily.

"No, young man," the preacher called down from the platform. "God can meet with you. I am going to give you four divine principles. You work on them; but you must be absolutely honest to yourself and to God. That is all you need to do, and the One who has written these promises will fulfill them."

I can't count the times in the years since that I have shared the same four principles with a hurting man or woman. I still marvel at their power, simplicity and irrefutable truth. Four simple statements encompass the mystery of salvation and herald the total transformation of the most rebellious, God-hating, selfish soul into a child of the Creator.

1. Accept that you are a sinner, for "all have sinned, and come short of the glory of God" (Romans 3:23).

2. Remember that only Jesus Christ can forgive you. "If we confess our sins, he is faithful and just to forgive us our sins, and to cleanse us from all unrighteousness" (1 John 1:9).

3. No detergent can cleanse your heart, "But if we walk in the light, as he is in the light, we have fellowship one with another, and the blood of Jesus Christ his Son cleanseth us from all sin" (1 John 1:7).

4. Open wide the doors of your heart and welcome

the Lord Jesus Christ into your life. "But as many as received him, to them gave he power to become the sons of God, even to them that believe on His name" (John 1:12).

Listening to that God-inspired minister that day, I realized I had heard these truths many times before. In a hundred different ways my parents had drilled these principles into me. Now I was standing at a moment of decision. A spiritual battle was being waged in my mind. Part of me was still gripped with a spirit of rebellion.

Well, he told me to be honest, I thought. *I am going to end my life anyway. What can it hurt to tell these people how I really feel? My embarrassment will be short-lived.*

"All right," I said, looking up at the evangelist and the Sinhala interpreter. "I'll be honest. I'll think about what you've just said. But if it does not work, will you allow me to go onto the platform, take the microphone and tell all these young people that this is all a lie?"

The preacher shocked me. He had such conviction of the power of the truths he had just shared with me. "Sure, young man," he said, "I'll give you that privilege."

He's accepted my challenge, I thought in triumph. Instead of kneeling, I placed both hands on a nearby chair and looked up to the roof of that auditorium. "God," I blurted, "I'm telling You for the second time, I don't believe You. You are not there. Nevertheless, this man says these are Your principles and You are going to work them out. He asked me to be honest, and I am going to be honest."

I paused. That same desperate prayer from the botanical garden sprang out of my mouth again. "If

You meet me now, I have nothing to offer You. But I will give You my life."

The Holy Spirit took over. The same Spirit who transformed my father and mother now took a loving grip on my heart. I felt His presence in a way I could never deny. This was not brainwashing. This was not parental propaganda. This was truth. This was power.

Suddenly I was sobbing, crying out to God with every fiber of my soul. I could no longer stand in arrogant belligerence. I crumbled to my knees, the tears running down my cheeks, down my neck, mixing with the sweat of my collar.

Time froze. When I finally stood up, it was like waking from a dream. Or, more accurately, it was like waking from a nightmare into a reassuring new reality. The crowd had returned to their seats. Both preachers stood there looking at me. Suddenly I could see the love of Christ in their smiles. That crowd of young people now appeared more as family members than strangers.

"Young man," the evangelist said in a peaceful tone, "you can go to the mic now. Tell the people what it's all about."

It was not an arrogant, angry teenage boy who jumped to the platform and grabbed the microphone. It was a humbled, tear-stained, redeemed sinner who had finally grown up. I slowly shuffled to the steps and meekly climbed them. I found my way to center stage before a hushed crowd.

"I don't know anything," I said to those young men and women in a voice that broke. "But, something has happened in my life." I told them a little about my experiences in the city. My past in all its folly now seemed so distant. God held my young life firmly to himself.

"I want to go home," I said in conclusion. "I must go and tell my parents what has happened."

Instantly the crowd erupted with rejoicing and praise. I let the microphone in my hand fall to my side as if surrendering my will to God. Then I closed my eyes and bowed my head in gratitude to a Savior who was taking me home.

A New Life

Appropriately dubbed the "black sheep" of my family, I had discarded the values of my parents and church. I had turned my back on my family in a culture that places great importance on the family unit. In Sri Lanka children often do not leave home even as married adults. So my running away was the ultimate slap in my parents' faces. Many young people in my position would have been too ashamed to return home. But I was a new person. What I desired most was to return to my family. *Even the Prodigal Son*, I thought as I reflected on my father's teaching from the Bible, *was determined to go home after he came to his right mind.*

It was late when the meeting at the YMCA was over. Now anxious to leave the city, I reached in my pocket searching for any remaining change I could use for bus fare. My hand wrapped around the bottle of poison. Suddenly it seemed like years ago, rather than that afternoon, that I had attempted to take my life. In disgust I pulled the bottle from my pocket and hurled it into the gutter.

I didn't waste any time. I caught a bus out of Colombo and headed home. Because of the late hour, I missed the connecting bus and had to walk the final four miles to Makevita. I had plenty of time to reflect yet again on the pain I had caused my parents. Despite my memories of their love and Christian faith, I wondered if they would welcome me back into our home or cast me out to face the consequences of my folly.

By the time I was within sight of our home, it was past midnight. The night wrapped itself around the house in a cool embrace that chased the day's heat away. Crickets and a myriad of other insects filled the air with their steady conversation. I hesitated because of the late hour. I could always sleep outside and face my parents in the morning. But something prodded me to go ahead and knock on the front door.

The light came on and the door was unlatched. I stood in the shadows, almost ready to run, still fearing rejection. Then, even before the door opened, I heard the voice of my mother.

"Colton, you have come back!"

I listened for any hint of anger or disapproval. All I heard was her love. Suddenly, I could hold back no longer. I stepped into the light, embraced my mother and held her as if I never wanted us to be apart again.

"Mummy," I finally stammered, "how did you know that I was standing outside the door?"

"Son," she said gently, "don't you know we have a prayer-hearing and prayer-answering God? He showed me you were returning."

There it was again—an unshakable faith that she and my father seemed to exhale with each breath.

"Let me tell you something more," she continued, this time with a note of authority in her voice. "You are not that same old Colton. You are a new boy."

I was startled. I had not said a word about why I had returned home. "How do you know that?" I asked in shock.

She smiled. "Your father and I told God, 'Don't send the old Colton through these doors again. But when You do send him, please send a new Colton home.'"

It suddenly became clear to me how my father and mother had spent the previous months. In my pride, I had envisioned them wringing their hands over me and giving me up to my own devices. I had fully intended to make a success of my life and then throw that success back in their faces. I would show them just how empty their superstitions were. But they had never cowered in fear or despair. They had taken hold of God's throne through the power of intercessory prayer. I was unknowingly a daily target of those prayers, caught squarely in those Divine crosshairs. There is no one who can pray so fervently for an errant child as a mother and a father who are committed to ensuring that such a rebel is brought back to God. My parents' prayers brought me back from the very edge of death and a Godless eternity.

"Can you forgive me?" I asked.

She didn't respond immediately. She simply pulled me to herself and patted my back, saying, "You're home and you're our son."

"Where is Daddy?" I asked.

"Sleeping," she said. "He didn't hear the door."

My trepidation reasserted itself. My offenses seemed all the greater now that I had to confess them again to my father. I walked quietly to his bedside trying to think of what to say first. All I could do was fall on him in sudden sorrow. "I'm sorry. I'm so sorry," I told him as he awoke. He took me in his arms. Our reunion was instant and complete.

My sorrow gave way to excitement. I was so thrilled about what God had done for me that I couldn't keep it inside. "Daddy," I said, "all I want to do is go out and tell every young man and young woman that God does miracles. He did such a miracle for me."

My father was wise. He let me talk of my dream of sharing the gospel then put his arm around me. "Son," he said, "that's wonderful. God has certainly touched your life. But even when God calls you, you need preparation.

If you want to share the gospel and preach, you must go to Bible school."

Of course, in those days Bible school meant I needed to learn English. I did not know much English at the time. I certainly couldn't speak, read or write it—all necessary skills for studying Bible courses at the school, because all the teaching was in English.

Mother fetched me some tea and a small meal. Then she put me to bed. I lay there in the dark, hardly believing I was home again. A lifetime had seemed to pass in the months I had been gone. Yet, it was almost as if I had never left. In a matter of hours God had restored me to my beloved family and filled my heart with peace.

That night I drifted off to sleep with a newfound purpose, sensing that a celebration was taking place in heaven because my life had been rescued for eternity. God was giving me a second chance to fulfill the destiny He had placed on my life before I was born.

CHAPTER 7

Sharing the Good News

I awoke to the sound of a bell. It was the grating metallic rasp of a bicycle bell. The old Colton would have pulled the covers over his head and tried to shut out the noise in pursuit of more sleep. The new Colton suddenly heard opportunity calling.

It was the paperboy, a young fellow who had ridden by our house hundreds of times and on down the gravel road with hardly a glance in our direction as he effortlessly flicked a newspaper onto our porch. But he didn't get away so easily that day. I ran outside and chased him down. I grabbed hold of his handlebars and brought him to a halt. He looked at me like I was insane (a look I would receive from quite a number of people in the years to come).

"I'm saved," I said excitedly. As I unfolded the story of my miracle, his shock and surprise soon turned to keen interest. I asked him to consider the same truths the evangelist had placed before me. Then we prayed together.

"Thank you for telling me your story," he said. "I have a peace inside." As he pedaled away, the bicycle bell no longer seemed to rasp. There was a spring in each pump he gave to his pedals. His life was changed.

I had hardly finished telling the paperboy my story when the bread man met me at our doorstep. He folded his arms and listened to the account of my transformation. My beaming face and animated gestures added life to my words. The change in me was undeniable. He let me pray with him.

"Sir," he said, "I felt a big burden roll off as you prayed."

"That is a miracle from God," I said.

"Do God's miracles include healing?" he asked. He told me he suffered from chronic bleeding ulcers.

I prayed again. God immediately healed him.

I then encountered a man trying to sell fresh fish and a woman selling vegetables. With a sense of urgency, I told them what Jesus Christ had done for me. I wanted them to accept Christ too.

"I have to be going," they each said.

"No," I blurted. "If you leave me without accepting Christ, you are going to spend eternity in hell." That was my conviction. I said, "You need Christ today." The paperboy and bread man had responded affirmatively, but the fishmonger and vegetable woman rejected their divine opportunity. At that moment, for the first time in my life, I grieved at the thought of people going to hell.

I didn't have theological knowledge, but I knew God was in the present. He makes no guarantees about there being a tomorrow. When God speaks, we must respond immediately; when He instructs us to do something, we must act today. For nearly 60 years now I have not stopped to worry how God would bring provision for a task at hand; I always saw the need, knew that God wanted me to address that need and plunged headlong into it.

I learned another lesson that day as I pleaded with those local friends—a lesson that had begun to make itself apparent to me when I stood in front of the audience at the YMCA. I was certainly no great orator. I did not yet have a deep understanding of God's Word. But I had a burning compulsion to tell others how Christ had given me new life. And when I obediently followed the impulse to share God's love, He stepped in and empowered my speech every time. Starting the following week I told nearly everyone I met in the village about my salvation. Though I was still a boy in their view, people began to come to me to hear my story and share the burden on their hearts.

That is how my ministry began. The simple reality of God's transforming touch on my life became the root of every sermon I preached, every prayer I offered on someone's behalf, and every illness or demonic oppression I confronted in the power of the Holy Spirit.

MY
ADVENTURE
IN FAITH

COLTON, SUSANNE (IN NIGERIAN DRESS) AT IMPETUS NIGERIA WITH ILA AND ELPHEGE FERNANDO, GERALD SENN AND SOME NIGERIAN DELEGATES.

Rejected

God answered prayer whenever I told my story and prayed for people in need. Occasionally I missed school because I was praying for someone. I was consumed with the desire to fulfill God's call on my life. School, food, sleep became less important.

But in time I discovered that I had less and less to offer people. I realized the wisdom of my father's advice: I needed to study the Bible systematically in an environment that would nurture my call and prod me along my spiritual journey. But I still did not know English, which was necessary to study at the Bible school operated by the Assemblies of God.

I decided not to let that obstacle stand in the way. I went to a friend in the village who knew English very well. I asked him to write an application letter for me to the Bible school, informing them that I had experienced a miracle, that God wanted me to preach and therefore I wanted to study the Bible at their institution. I mailed the letter and waited with confidence for the school's invitation to enroll.

I received a prompt reply. I tore open the envelope and took the letter immediately to my friend so he could read me the good news. He glanced at the page, grimaced a bit in my direction, then looked back at the page.

"Well," I prodded, "when do they want me to be ready for classes?"

"Colton . . ." he stammered, "the letter says . . ."

"Quit mumbling and read it," I told him.

"As you wish. 'We received your application and rejoice with you at the touch of God on your life. However, we are very sorry, but you do not meet the qualifications and we cannot admit you to Bible school.' " He reluctantly explained to me the contents of the letter.

I was stunned, but quickly recovered. They were just testing me to see how badly I wanted to come to their school, I thought. I convinced my friend to write a second letter of application.

Before long another response from the Bible school informed me the faculty unanimously decided I could not be enrolled. The stated reason—my lack of proficiency in English.

I took those two letters and went to my bedroom with a heavy heart. I placed them on my bed facing the window. "God," I prayed, "take a good look at these two letters. The principal and faculty are working against Your will."

Convinced that God would quickly rectify the situation, I went back to my friend. My insistence might sound naïve, but I was simply exercising the same unrelenting faith I had seen exhibited by my parents. Never give up. Never say it cannot be done. If you are moving in God's plan, there is no man on earth, no force in the universe, no demon in hell that can frustrate or destroy the plan of God concerning you.

"Write another application," I said to my friend. He started to protest, then shook his head and put pen to paper to write to the principal directly.

"Dear Brother in Christ," I dictated. "I have had a miracle. I am a new creation. Can you match anything with that? Can you compare anything with the miracle of your salvation? You have received the promise of eternal life. As I too have received this miracle, I want to study the Bible. Qualifications: Since my last letter I have been baptized in the Holy Spirit and have spoken in an unknown language. I believe it is a heavenly language. If God the Holy Spirit can give me an angelic language, surely, the Holy Spirit can teach me English. After all, what is English? A language spoken by every Tom, Dick and Harry on the streets."

I sent the application. But this time I did not receive a reply.

Kneeling next to my bed one night, I said, "Lord, You must make a way. I have done all I can. Now it's in Your hands."

MY ADVENTURE IN FAITH

AFTER RECEIVING HIS DOCTORATE FROM SOUTHERN
CALIFORNIA COLLEGE IN MARCH 1972.

Simple Faith

When I heard that the principal of the Bible school would be preaching in my village, I eagerly anticipated meeting him face to face.

Missionary Carl F. Graves, a great man of God, was preaching that day with an interpreter. I sat in front and took in every word. In strident tones, I responded with "Hallelujah," "Praise the Lord," and "Amen." There was no way that Bible school principal could miss me; I was seated right under his nose and I was the loudest member of the audience.

At the close of the message, Brother Graves came down with the interpreter and spoke with me.

"Colton, are you still of the persuasion that you want to go to Bible school?" he asked with some amazement.

"Sure I am," I said. "I want to go."

"Well, we have already started school, but I'm willing to try you out," he said, to my immediate joy and amazement. "I'll give you six months' probation."

"Brother Graves, that's just enough," I said. "Six months is all that I need." My enthusiasm was not dampened in the least by the fact I had to speak to him in Sinhala.

"Then you must come right away with me to the Bible school," he announced.

I ran home in a fever of surprise and excitement to pack my only two pairs of pants and two shirts for the trip.

"Colton, what are you doing?" my mother asked.

"Mummy," I announced, "I'm going to Bible school!"

"When are you going?" she asked.

"Mummy, today is the day; now is the time. Tell Daddy that I will see him soon and that I love him."

Brother Graves pulled up in front of our house. I quickly embraced my mother, then took my suitcase and ran to the car. I was off to Bible school.

The mad rush of that afternoon helped imprint another spiritual practice in my life. Never put things off. When you know God is leading you to act, do not delay. You may never hear that voice a second time. "Obedience is better than sacrifice," the prophet Samuel told Israel's first king, Saul. It is also certainly better than delay. God does not adjust His timetable to our actions either. Yes, we must obey immediately when we hear His voice. But He continues to work His processes in us on His own heavenly schedule.

I found myself at Bible school but quickly realized God was going to have to do some radical things in me if I was to last longer than six months. Despite my ignorance of English and having been reminded numerous times the class lectures were delivered in that language, I had still expected to be able to fit in and participate. To my dismay, everything the teachers said might as well have been in Greek. I didn't understand a word of it. Monday it was Greek. Tuesday it was Greek. Wednesday it was Greek. By Thursday, I made my way back to my dormitory utterly frustrated.

We were not allowed to have a light on after 10 p.m. The only place where we could have a light was in the bathroom. So on Thursday I got a wild idea. I took my English Bible and my Sinhala Bible and locked myself in the bathroom. With a Bible open on each knee, I prayed.

"God," I said, "I kept my part of the contract. Now it's up to You to fulfill Yours."

I never took one English lesson. On the strength of faith, I learned English at the age of 18. That humble bathroom was my classroom. Over time, as I prayerfully devoured the Word of God, the eternal truths from the Sinhala Bible began to find their parallels in my English Bible. It was as if God had opened my ears to the English language; my classes began to yield meaning.

God taught me another lifelong spiritual principle through His English lessons: The equipment to do God's work is from the Lord. Our warfare is spiritual. We can't rely on talent alone. Our ability and all that we need come from Him. Far beyond any initial reservoir of ability He creates in us, He is able to further equip us for any task. We never need to question whether we are suitable candidates for something God asks us to do. We become suitable because the Holy Spirit gives us all we need to complete His work.

Eventually I completed my six months' probation and the faculty decided to give me another six months. I decided it was an honor to be "God's probation student." Permanence and security can become the enemy of faith. That's where many people miss a blessing. Abraham, even in the land of promise, considered himself to be a pilgrim. He was just moving through Canaan relying on God's direction day by day. That's what God wants us to do. That's what God was teaching me in His divine school even while I toiled in that Bible school's classrooms.

MY ADVENTURE IN FAITH

COLTON'S FATHER, SAM WICKRAMARATNE.

Gathering Clouds

1951. I was about to enter my second year of Bible school. And now that I understood English I was making great strides academically. I was looking forward to the next year of study. Then my father died.

Short, stout Sam Wickramaratne had seemed indestructible. The one-time customs officer who pastored a small village congregation had completed his life's mission and God had called him home. It reminded me that God doesn't judge us on how many days we live—He judges us on how we spend our days. And my father spent his days well.

I participated in the funeral and comforted my mother before returning to the Bible school. I knew my father would want me to quickly return to my studies. But the most pressing issue I faced was my tuition fees, which my father had previously paid. Now it was up to me to find a way.

But I had no source of income. My tuition fees were due at the end of every month. Every spare moment was spent in prayer, pleading with God, "Lord, raise up someone to pay my fees."

My tuition fees were due in three days so I requested three days' leave from Sister Graves to fast and pray.

Our school was close to the sea. I used to go to the shore every morning and sit on a particular rock and meditate and pray. Then I would get up and walk along the beach to a certain point and back, and I would sense a Presence walking with me. Years later, especially when facing a crisis, I would return to that spot to seek the face of God.

One morning I went to the rock, greatly burdened. I could smell the salt in the air. Gulls and other sea birds flew patterns in the sky. The surf crashed against the rocks in a timeless melody. All around me was ample evidence of the power of the One who created me, the One who saved my soul from self-destruction and the One who was guiding my steps in His service. As I waited on Him in prayer, the sun journeyed from horizon to horizon, at first offering gentle warmth, then engulfing me in its daily crescendo of strength before setting and surrendering the coast to the cool of a starry evening. I had not tasted food all day. I was convinced that my fasting and prayers would be met with God's solution to my tuition crisis.

But when I returned to my dormitory that evening, I found God's answer was understated to the point of silence. Despite my expectations, no one had written a letter with the needed funds enclosed. I awakened early the next morning and returned to the rock. Again, a day's worth of prayer and fasting revealed no answer. Heading back to my dormitory that night, exhausted from three days of concerted prayer and self-denial, my heart broke.

"God," I prayed in the gathering darkness, "there's nobody to support me. Tomorrow my fees are due. Lord, if You want me to leave and go and be a good deacon in a church and support this school—all right. If that's Your plan, I'll pack my bags and tomorrow I will walk out of this school and get a job. I promise You that I'll send half of my salary to this school to support someone in my place."

But my offer was made out of heartache. I could not understand why God would allow me to come this far, on what seemed to be a divinely chosen path only to be stopped short by an insurmountable financial wall. Tearfully I tiptoed upstairs to spend what I thought was my last night in this room.

I noticed a strip of paper on my bed—a message from the principal: "The principal wishes to see you the moment you arrive."

Meetings with the principal were never good.

"Dear Lord," I prayed, "what have I done? Tomorrow I have to leave school and I'm already in for trouble."

I quickly ran down and tapped on the Graveses' door.

"Sister Graves," I said as she answered my knock, "Brother Graves wants to see me."

She gave me no indication as to why he wanted to see me. She offered no reassurance. She simply said, "Not tonight, tomorrow after breakfast."

I returned to my room only to have the longest night of my life. I couldn't sleep. I took an inventory of my life and searched my heart, wondering if there was something in my life that had brought God's judgment on me. But I could find nothing to confess. Although I could not understand it, I had to conclude God had a different plan for my life than Bible college.

The following morning I went to the breakfast table and my nerves were so worn that, despite my three-day fast, I couldn't eat a morsel of food. My stomach was in knots and disappointment and discouragement clung to my face like an uncomfortable mask. This was the morning that would change my life—one way or the other.

MY ADVENTURE IN FAITH

CARL AND BERTHA GRAVES, THE CEYLON BIBLE INSTITUTE
PRINCIPAL AND WIFE.

A Widow's Sacrifice

On an empty and nervous stomach, I found myself standing by the principal's door. I was shivering like a leaf in a storm because no one was called to Brother Graves' office for trivial reasons. Whatever it was—was serious.

Brother Graves walked into his office, smiled, then motioned for me to take a seat. He handed me an envelope.

"Money?" I asked.

"That's your pocket money," he replied.

"Pocket money? I haven't even paid my fees yet," I said.

He grinned. "Go ahead and read the letter."

The first letter was written to the Assemblies of God headquarters in Springfield, Missouri.

Dear Brethren,
You will be surprised to receive this letter. I am a poor widow living in Panama City, Florida. When I was in prayer, God spoke to me and said, "There's a place called Ceylon. There's a Bible School and there's a student there that you must support."
I went to the world map that is hanging on my wall and searched and searched but I could find no place called Ceylon. If you know of a place called Ceylon, will you

please send me the name and the address of the Bible School?

Florence Pokorney

Brother Graves handed me a second letter.

The Principal, Ceylon Bible Institute
15, Melbourne Avenue
Colombo 4, Ceylon

Dear Brother in Christ,

You'll be surprised to receive this letter. I am a poor widow living in Panama City, Florida. I live by scrubbing floors, mending clothes and cutting lawns for other people, but God spoke to me when I was in prayer. He said, "There is a student in Ceylon and I want you to support that student."
I don't have much money but I'm sending the little I have.

Florence Pokorney

Sister Pokorney didn't even write a check. She had enclosed American currency and it was a miracle the cash came intact through two nations' postal departments. Her gift arrived right on time. Brother Graves designated some of the money for my tuition and gave me what remained. God is never late. He is never early. He is always on time.

The Lord has said, "I will never leave thee, nor forsake thee" (Hebrews 13:5). He has promised, "I am with you alway, even unto the end of the world" (Matthew 28:20). Why do we doubt? Why do we wonder if He hears us? He is always with us. We are never alone. But in this instance I had allowed doubt to fill my mind—questioning whether God would take care of my tuition. In His time, in His way, His provision came.

I began to write to this dear woman in Panama City. As we corresponded I gained a deeper insight into the sacrifice God was calling her to make. "Colton," she said, "I have cut back on my meat, eggs and milk to send you this money."

Once she wrote to me, "Son, my bedroom roof is leaking. But I won't send a man up to repair it. If I do I can't send you these few dollars. I'm pushing my bed into the living room."

Each time I would take a little toothpaste to brush my teeth, I would cry at the realization I was living on the money of a poor widow. Just as God used a widow to meet Elijah's need, He had sent a widow to meet mine.

Through this experience I learned a lesson that would remain with me to this day: We believe our provision must come from resources we have identified and we think God must use, but God's ways are mysterious and glorious. When we pray about a need, it is not for us to tell Him how to provide; we simply submit our need to Him and rest in the confidence of His provision.

The Bible says that Jesus, our High Priest, is "touched with the feeling of our infirmities" (Hebrews 4:15). There are deep-rooted matters in our lives that we can't share even with those who are closest to us. But God is touched by those needs. He is mindful of them. He is not distant or preoccupied. We are in His sights. He will bring us through.

MY ADVENTURE IN FAITH

DEDICATION OF THE CHURCH AT THE FORMER STABLE AT ALWIS PLACE .

CHAPTER 12

Lessons, Lessons, Lessons

The teachings of Jesus are practical. They relate to everyday living. If a person wants to live right and make good decisions, he or she must know the Word of God. John 8:32 says, "Ye shall know the truth, and the truth shall make you free." Our duty is to learn the truth, proclaim it, contend for it and live it. That is all you need to do. When God's Word is proclaimed, "It shall accomplish" (Isaiah 55:11). We don't have to alter, amplify or add to it. But the process of learning before proclaiming can be painful.

One day I had to preach in a chapel service at the Bible college. I owned only two shirts—and both had gaping holes in the back. So I took a pair of scissors and cut the back out of one. I had only the front portion, which I wore with a tie. I borrowed a jacket from one of my colleagues. Even my trousers were patched. I put cardboard in my shoes to fill the holes in the soles.

I felt sorry for myself. "Lord," I prayed, "I am Your servant. Here I am wearing a shirt without a back and a borrowed coat."

But the Lord spoke to me. "Are you going to be My man because you have clothes, money and fame? Or, are you going to serve Me because I am everything to you?"

I felt the Holy Spirit's conviction. "Yes, Lord," I said,

"You are God."

It was a moment of personal brokenness, but out of it I stepped up to preach with a fresh anointing. The power of God was evident in my voice. I began to prophesy and proclaim that God would do great and mighty things. I told the students God was going to take me around the world and thousands of rupees would pass through my hands for the work of God.

The faculty and students were angry, thinking I had become arrogant and full of ambition. I was escorted into the staff room at the close of the chapel service.

Then the principal and staff gave me a good dressing down. They said, "You are talking too big. Do you think the other students have no faith? They have more faith than you."

They knew that I was wearing a borrowed coat to cover my shirt that had no back. I was standing behind a mirror and they placed another mirror in front of me and said, "Man of Faith, remove your coat."

I pulled off my coat, revealing my bare back. Tears began to stream down my cheeks.

"Brothers," I said, "with all due respect to you, I want you to know I don't preach the gospel because of the clothes I wear or the money I have or the status I have received. I preach the gospel because God is God and there is none beside Him. The day will come if you and I live that these very prophecies will be fulfilled."

Some time later one of the faculty members put his arms around me and said, "Colton, I am sorry. I can see God in you. We misjudged you."

At the time, though, I didn't understand the criticism, but it helped shape me into a man of God who doesn't boast in himself. God was trying to teach me that it is easy for any of us to be His chosen vessel and yet move or react in ways that are out of His will. Think of Moses. God saved him. God delivered him from the jaws of death in the Nile River. He was destined to be Israel's deliverer. But he didn't act like God's chosen servant when he saw an Egyptian beating one of his countrymen. He responded by taking the Egyptian's life and hiding his evil deed by burying the body in the sand (Exodus 2:11-12). We can be God's servants and know what God wants us to do, and yet do it in the wrong way. As a result, we dishonor God's name.

It was obvious I still had much to learn. So, I studied textbooks in the physical classroom and listened for God's voice in the classroom of the Holy Spirit. "Being God's man or woman won't make you a popular person," the Spirit would remind me. God's person-in-training is often lonely, because sometimes He wants us to press on alone to nurture greater reliance on Him. It is easy to drift downstream with the other fish, but sometimes God wants us to swim against the current of public opinion. That can be a lonely and costly place. But men and women of God are committed to following the leading of the Spirit moment by moment, regardless of the price. They know His Word acted out in their lives, in His time, in His way, will always bring about His results.

MY ADVENTURE IN FAITH

SUSANNE, THE GIRL COLTON HAD SEEN IN A HOSPITAL BED.

My Life Partner

In Bible school the more I learned from God's Word the more zealous I was to put faith into practice. Opportunities to preach were few as our organization had only one church in the city, the Colombo Gospel Tabernacle. We had to preach on street corners to crowds that were always on the move. Christ's compassion and love were compelling me, and I seized every opportunity to preach anywhere, at any time. I had a burning desire to see the acts of the Holy Spirit repeated in and through my life.

Since the day I had prayed for the breadman's healing in our village, the Lord had burdened me for the needs of the sick. I wanted to see God heal miraculously, so I decided to visit the local hospitals with a fellow student every week, to pray for the sick and suffering. How God blessed those times—we saw one healing after another and those miracles built a fire under our faith. And little did I know God was using that ministry to perform a life-changing miracle for me.

One evening as we were walking through the wards of a hospital we saw a young girl weak and helpless on a bed. We offered to pray for her. She declined. So we stepped back.

The Spirit spoke a word of urgency to me as we turned to walk away. "If that girl dies," I told my friend, "we'll be partly to blame. Let's ask her again if we can pray for her."

She was still reluctant, but finally nodded her approval.

As we exited the hospital that night—after praying for her—I turned to my friend and said something that still makes me smile with amazement: "Supposing this girl gets saved and healed. Who knows, she might become my wife."

"Don't talk that kind of nonsense," he replied.

But those were not idle words that night. That young girl, Susanne, received her healing.

A short time later, influenced by her older brother Elphege, Susanne came to the Colombo Gospel Tabernacle and God saved her. I saw her singing in the choir and told my buddies that she would one day be my wife. My excitement was short-lived as one of my friends said, "Lay off. She is already taken."

A few months later, I was asked to preach at a youth camp. When I learned Susanne was upset over her broken relationship, I consoled her by saying, "Don't worry, silver shall be replaced with gold."

On the last day of the camp we all climbed a nearby mountain. On the peak of that mountain God spoke clearly to Susanne and me that He would bring us together in life and in ministry. One day I would be her "gold."

Circumstances and time do not frustrate God's plan. The waiting and suffering can never be compared with the compensation I received in Susanne. He that "findeth a wife findeth a good thing" (Proverbs 18:22). It is not easy to find a virtuous woman. She is far more valuable than the most precious stones on earth (Proverbs 31:10). Besides my precious salvation and the gift of the Holy Spirit, Susanne is the greatest gift God could have ever given to me.

Launching Into Ministry

When I stepped up to the podium as graduation speaker at the Ceylon Bible Institute in 1953, it was a testimony of God's grace and power. He had taught me English and strengthened me academically. And He had sustained me from month to month on the sacrificial offerings of a Florida widow. But God was still sanding down the rough edges of my nature. My fervor for God had caused some to mislabel me as a rebel.

After graduation I simply went home to pray and seek God's direction for my life and ministry. In times of decision like this, God often beckons us to get alone with Him. Most people don't like to be alone because during solitude they are reminded of the things they don't like about themselves. But it is at such times that you meet God. The Holy Spirit sent Jesus into the wilderness because it was there, alone, that He was prepared for His ministry (Mark 1:12-14). Alone, we can begin to realize our complete need for the Lord. Then we begin to seek Him with our whole heart, creating the very conditions by which He promises to be found (Jeremiah 29:13).

During periods of being alone, doubts can arise. We begin to wonder if we are hearing from God and following His instructions. But even when we don't understand ourselves it is comforting to know God understands us.

Though we may find ourselves in a dark place, God says, "Seek and you shall find." He is right there—even in the dark and lonely times. He is always standing in front of us, but sometimes we allow circumstances to put a mythical veil between us. He's saying, "Come, come," and we say, "Lord, I'm seeking You, but I can't see You." When He embraces us, we reply, "I found You, I found You." But that's really not what happened. He was right there all along and finally we walked into His waiting arms.

I graduated from Bible college in March 1953. Even though I had been selected as the graduation speaker, I found myself back home in Makevita without a church appointment. However, the people in my father's church were pleased to see me, and in July 1953 I was appointed pastor of the church under a missionary. But my spirit was restless. I sensed God didn't want me to grow too comfortable.

In 1954 some Swedish Pentecostals were beginning to evangelize in the up-country area. They asked me to preach for them at a small revival meeting. In preparation, I prayed until I believed I was in a place where the Holy Spirit could minister through me. Night after night, as I preached, a conviction grew in my spirit—almost like an ever-increasing wave. I told the people to bring the deaf and the dumb to the next service. God was going to do a miracle.

The following day when I was about to preach there was a disruption. Some unbelievers brought a young man who had been deaf and mute from birth. For years he had begged on the streets. They pushed him to the front and confronted me: "You said God can do any miracle, so now let's see Him heal this boy."

The Swedish missionaries and preachers were all seated

behind me on the tiny platform. I could hear their prayers, "Oh God, Colton is very exuberant and enthusiastic. Now, Lord, save us . . ." It was like a cold chill behind me, rather than a fire of faith. I knew I needed to clear the platform of whatever would cause my faith to waver, but they were the leaders of the crusade and I didn't want to show disrespect. So I requested that they move to the front row of seats. They complied.

Then I turned to the people who had brought the boy. "Look here," I said, "when you go to a doctor, you don't tell him what he should do. He gives you the prescription and you obey him. I have a prescription and you will stand there until I finish giving you my prescription." I promptly preached a salvation message and gave an altar call. Many came forward to receive Christ for the first time; others rededicated their lives to the Lord.

But the deaf-mute still stood locked in his prison of silence.

I called for others with hearing problems to come forward for prayer. And when God healed them, my faith grew.

I spoke directly to the ones who had brought the deaf boy. "All of you—come. You must give your lives to Jesus. I can't heal. Only Jesus heals."

They protested.

"This is the prescription. If you want it, this is the way." Although I wasn't convinced of their commitment, I led them in the sinner's prayer.

Then the moment of truth came. I felt the weight of each person's gaze—the perplexed glares of believers and the leers of those bound by false faith and intent on proving mine a lie.

The deaf-mute sat in a chair in front of me. I put my fingers in the boy's ears and prayed. With my final amen, every hearing person in that meeting could have heard the proverbial pin drop. I looked at the boy; he looked at me.

In those days we still had spring-loaded watches that ticked. I placed my watch next to his ear. There was a pause, a questioning look on his face. Suddenly, he jumped up. I knew God had healed him.

I prayed for his vocal cords. "Oh, God," I said with a voice aimed at that crowd as much as it was directed to the Lord, "make him speak."

I turned to the boy. "I want you to say something for me." He nodded, still taken aback that he could hear my request without trying to read my lips. I told him to repeat the words after me: "I love Jesus."

"I love Jesus," he said quietly. "I love Jesus," he repeated with more conviction.

Then I stepped off the platform and walked down the aisle. I shouted back to him, "I love Jesus." He joyfully repeated my cry.

The crowd exploded with praise and rejoiced in the miracle. It was like a scene from the Book of Acts. Instead of a lifelong lame beggar leaping for joy, here was a lifelong deaf and mute beggar shouting his love for Jesus.

The unbelieving people who had brought the boy to the meeting to discredit me were speechless. They could not deny what God had done in the boy's life. God had turned the situation around, confirmed His Word and protected His servant.

The Road to Kandy and Being God's Misunderstood Man

As I finished a revival meeting one night I was handed a telegram. It was from Brother Graves informing me that the Assemblies of God Executive Committee wanted to see me at 9:00 the next morning. I showed the message to my Swedish friends.

"Colton," they said, "you can't go now. You are the evangelist for these meetings and we have had this miracle. Tomorrow, we are going to have even greater crowds as word spreads about the healings that took place. Please postpone this trip."

"This is from my General Superintendent and the Executive Committee," I explained. "If they want me tomorrow, I must go."

On the overnight train to Colombo, I pondered the telegram. The committee must have heard how God was using me at the evangelistic crusade, I decided. They must have a special assignment for me—perhaps a promotion. Hope welled up within me. I could never have imagined what was to follow.

When I arrived I was handed a piece of paper and asked to wait in an adjoining room. Pain rushed through me when I read what was on the paper. Someone had compiled a list of charges against me.

"Dear Lord," I prayed, "even when I was a sinner, I didn't commit these sins. Now I am being charged by my own brethren."

Among the nine charges was one accusing Susanne, my future wife, and me of immoral behavior. As I read the accusations I became furious. I was ready to give the committee a piece of my mind. I was ready to slam my fist on the table in defense of my reputation and to sue them for defamation of character.

But a gentle voice quieted my spirit. *What would Jesus do? When He was taken to judgment, "as a sheep before her shearers is dumb, so he openth not his mouth."* When I was finally called into the next room, I resisted the urge to lash out and stood quietly before the committee.

Brother Graves was somber. "Colton," he said, "have you read these charges?"

"Yes," I said stoically.

"Are they true?" he asked.

My rage was gone. God's peace had taken control. "Brethren," I said, "before God and before you, I want to tell you that I am not guilty of any of these charges. But whatever punishment you mete out I'll accept because God has placed you above me."

Though they were on the verge of dismissing me from the ministry, my attitude alone cast doubt on the accusations brought against me. They asked me to wait outside while they conferred.

Bill Farrand, a young missionary who had recently come to Sri Lanka from Michigan, was a member of the committee. He stood and spoke on my behalf.

"Give that young man to me," he offered. "I need someone to help me in Kandy."

The committee reluctantly agreed. I was assigned to work under Brother Farrand in the town of Kandy, in the very heart of Sri Lanka. I would be on probation and was not to have contact with Susanne or travel without permission. And my ministerial credentials were temporarily revoked.

I felt the punishment was extremely harsh for what amounted to unsubstantiated accusations, but the Holy Spirit continued to soften my heart and guide my response. I told the brethren I would accept their conditions.

I met with Susanne and told her it would be the last time we could see each other until this misunderstanding had passed.

"Colton," she said, "God revealed to me that He would take you to Kandy. You be obedient to God. Don't worry, just go."

On my way to Makevita, I was wondering how to break the news to my mother and sister that I had to leave immediately for Kandy. When I saw my mother I spoke a word of faith: "Mummy, I have got a promotion. Out of all the ministers, the executive committee has assigned me to go and work with the new missionary in Kandy."

I bid farewell to my mother and sister and told our family church I would no longer be able to be their pastor.

With all the arrangements in place, I sat in the backseat of the Farrands' car headed to Kandy. I was crestfallen. This was not how I had planned to begin my ministry. I had no ministerial credentials. I had been openly accused of terrible impropriety. The most personal relationships in my life were now disrupted. But God was about to show me His plan hidden beneath the unpleasant veneer of the past day's events.

There is still a landmark I can show anyone who travels with me on that road to Kandy. It's about 35 miles inland from Colombo. It's the spot where the Farrands first showed me the kind of godly mentors they would be in my life.

I had been sitting in the back of the car in silent discouragement when suddenly the car stopped. Brother Farrand turned to his wife and said, "Alvera, would you mind sitting in the back? I need to talk with Colton." Then he turned to me with a smile. "Colton, come up front."

I wasn't sure what he thought of the proceedings and the charges levied against me.

"Buddy, listen to me," he said. "You are not going to Kandy as some sort of punishment. You are my associate pastor. I trust you. You have permission to write as many letters as you want to Susanne."

We drove the rest of the way to Kandy talking like friends. When we arrived, I discovered that Brother Farrand had called ahead and the fledgling church had prepared a banquet to welcome me.

In the end, despite all appearances to the contrary, these circumstances had not brought about my downfall. God, true to His word, had worked it all out for my good.

God used those difficult circumstances to nurture a submissive spirit in me. Jesus himself said He did not come to be served, but to serve (Matthew 20:28). If my Savior was willing to humble himself for people who eventually killed Him, how could I do anything else but follow

His example? God, in His time, blessed my ministry. I eventually served as General Superintendent for 26 years, leading the executive committee that had once entertained the accusations against me. God brought restoration where I once could see only repression.

One of the most difficult challenges a Christian minister faces is being misjudged and misunderstood. Many years later, as my ministry was being established and I could see what the Lord had shown me beginning to come to pass in a marvelous way, I was suddenly engulfed in a cloud of misunderstanding even though at that time I was in a position of leadership. As Jesus was silent before His accusers, I had to quietly stand by as the clouds continued to billow around me. It took the grace of God and His divine enabling to maintain a spirit of forgiveness and love and to restrain even those close to me from any form of retaliation. In God's good time He vindicated me and in His time He brought reconciliation, restoration of fellowship, and love among us.

Once again, as I was about to resign from the leadership of the Assemblies of God fellowship, a position I had held continuously for over 35 years—as secretary, vice chairman, and then chairman for 24 years, I found myself being falsely maligned and misjudged. At such times, strength comes from being guiltless before the Lord and in the quiet confidence that He is your Defender. The Lord made manifest my innocence and my name and testimony were left untarnished.

In such times of testing, when you are faced with the temptation to retaliate in indignation, remember that the Lord who called you to serve Him will deal with every situation with justice. If we commit our way to the Lord and wait on Him, He will make all things right and beautiful in His time!

MY ADVENTURE IN FAITH

MISSIONARY
MENTORS BILL
AND ALVERA
FARRAND.

CHAPTER 16

A Time of Mentoring

My studies in the school of the Spirit included some one-on-one sessions at Bill and Alvera Farrand's dinner table. Their strong faith reminded me of what I had witnessed in the lives of my parents.

"Colton," he would say, "tell me about that brother you visited in the hospital." Or, "Colton, how are your sermon notes coming along for next Sunday night?"

Our talks often would lead to a discussion of God's Word. Brother Farrand would offer insight, and would gently correct my assumptions when needed. Many times, those conversations would stretch through the evening. I remember occasions when we talked through the night. God had made Brother Farrand into the man he was, and he was willing to be used of God to share those insights with me. It has always been my desire to perpetuate his generous spirit to other young men and women who are filling the ranks of ministry today.

God does not produce spiritual leaders in an assembly line. He uses a wide range of challenging circumstances to shape them for His service. For me, the cloud under which I had originally come to Kandy continued to torment my spirit. God was testing and molding me through the ordeal and everything within me wanted to find a way to escape. I wanted to run, but God wanted me to persevere so I would learn His lessons well.

The Spirit of the Lord has to lead us to His school, and that school is not necessarily some exclusive academy. The Spirit of God led Jesus into the wilderness. Most people don't like to enter the wilderness. It is filled with uncertainty and insecurity. But it is in the wilderness that the Lord teaches us how to overcome.

Consider the temptations Jesus faced. If He did what Satan asked He would have exalted himself in the natural eye as the Son of God. But Jesus rebuked Satan, because He already knew He was the Son of God. He didn't have to prove it by turning stones into bread. It is in the wilderness that we learn to follow that example. We don't strive to prove ourselves. We trust God to prove himself through us.

As we grow as spiritual leaders we learn to recognize the difference between an organization and an organism. We learn that our position within a denomination or organization isn't as vital as our commitment to the well-being of the organism. The organization is really to be for the benefit of the organism—the true, living body of Christ. But we often get this backwards, making the organization take precedence over the organism. In other words, nurturing people and winning people to Christ can become secondary to sustaining an organization. We end up with a form of godliness, as the Bible says, without the blessing that comes from following the leading of the Holy Spirit.

Leaders are made in the school of the Spirit. Leadership is not just a matter of absorbing ideas, methodologies, strategies and principles. We must surrender ourselves to God. God will not step over the boundary of our sovereign will. He only knocks at the door. It's up to us to open it for Him. Anyone who is willing to open that door and study in the school of the Spirit can be used by God in a significant way.

The school of the Spirit takes us to the wilderness. The school of the Spirit includes seasons of suffering. Paul says we must know the fellowship of Christ's suffering as well as the power of the Resurrection (Philippians 3:10). Even Jesus Christ was made perfect through His suffering (Hebrews 2:10). There is a place for suffering because that is where you nail self to the cross.

Sanctification is a process. That's why Paul says we are to be a living sacrifice (Romans 12:1). He says, "I die daily" (1 Corinthians 15:31). Our emotions and attitudes have to be dealt with daily. But God doesn't do this by some force of divine will. We have to exercise our will in obedience to His Word.

Bill and Alvera Farrand lived out these principles before me every day I ministered with them. Yes, the church in Kandy was an organization. But the Farrands never lost sight of the concept of a living organism—the local body of Christ they were nurturing. Their ministry breathed life into spiritually hungry men and women, including me.

In the years that followed, their example of faith and their understanding of God's priorities helped me overcome obstacles that would threaten my ministry.

MY ADVENTURE IN FAITH

COLTON AND SUSANNE'S WEDDING.

A Wedding, a Miracle, and a Car

In 1955 Susanne and I made plans to marry. Her Roman Catholic family didn't approve because I was a Protestant and, in fact, most of them did not even attend our wedding. But Susanne and I knew God had brought us together and we prayed that eventually He would unite our families. Over the years, one by one, God honored that prayer.

Brother Graves and missionary Harold Kohl conducted the ceremony. It was no lavish event. We didn't have money to buy expensive rings, hire a car or have a basic honeymoon. We had decided not to start life by taking a loan or getting into debt. We didn't even have a reception or wedding cake. But none of that mattered. Susanne and I were finally united, ready to face the world as Great Commission partners.

Soon afterwards, the Farrands left Kandy and I became the first Sri Lankan to succeed a missionary in an established church. The Farrands were pleased because, young as I was, the church services continued to be packed. I worked hard to build the church even though the salary was meager.

A significant miracle took place at this time. My mother always talked to God and reminded Him of His promise. "Lord," she would pray, "Your Word says, 'Believe on the Lord Jesus Christ, and thou shalt be saved, and thy house.' Lord, this means my seven boys and my girl—they all must get saved."

All my life I had heard this prayer. She persisted in prayer and one by one, with the exception of two of my brothers, we accepted the Lord Jesus.

When the time of her departure was at hand, Mother prayed the same prayer, saying, "Lord, before I leave this earth I want to see my two boys saved."

One day while we were all in prayer around her sick bed, my mother slipped away into eternity. At that moment my two brothers started to repent and cry and seek God's salvation, but my mother was gone. She had prayed, "Lord, the desire of the righteous will be granted. I pray that You will fulfill Your promise."

When I knew she had died I said, "God, You can't do this to her. You must show her that her prayer was answered."

I carried my dead mother and prayed for her and put her back on the bed and God brought her back to life to see her two wayward boys accept Christ as their personal Savior. She lived for six more months.

One day she called my wife, Susanne, to be with her, as she was not feeling well. While praying with Susanne, she said, "It is time for me to go home, but please don't ask Colton to come, as he won't let me go." A little while later she took her flight to heaven, saying, "Jesus, Jesus."

God honors our faith when we pray according to His Word.

After my mother passed away, my sister, three younger brothers and two nieces were stranded. Susanne was quick to invite all of them to our home despite my hesitation. Six months after our wedding, we had an expanded family living in our home. The church would scrape together a few rupees for us but we were learning to live on faith rather than rely on a bank account. As our faith was stretched, God continued to meet our needs.

Susanne and I used to walk many miles in and around Kandy, visiting hospitals and parishioners' homes. One day we walked up a long hill to visit some believers. I became so weary on our return journey that discouragement began to arise in my spirit. It was a winding road. It was a hot day.

We sat down by the road and drank some water. About that time I looked up and saw the transportation of my dreams. One of the local English tea plantation superintendents drove by in an open two-seat Fiat. He seemed oblivious of the heat. He was dressed in white for a tennis match. Despite the wind, every hair seemed in place.

"God," I prayed, "Susanne and I are Your servants and we have walked all day. We have had little food. We have to walk much farther." At that moment, I felt the authority of Christ rise in me. I knew, through Christ, I had the power to ask and receive His help in any situation.

My eyes widened with admiration as that two-seater drove by. We had no children so I knew it would be the perfect car for us at the time. I saw the license plate number, CL 7788.

"God," I said, "in the name of Jesus, today I claim *this* car to be my car." I didn't dwell on that car or allow it to consume my prayer life. I merely prayed and believed that God would have His way.

Some time later, Sister Rosa Reineker, a missionary, was left some money in her brother-in-law's will. God laid it on her heart to pay us a visit.

When she arrived, I offered my condolences.

"I heard about your loss," I said. "I'm sorry."

"Colton," she said, after taking a seat and accepting some tea, "God has given me some money, and I really thought for your faithfulness I might buy you a vehicle."

Susanne and I looked at each other. This was an answer to prayer. But we still had no idea how specific God's answer would be.

We visited a car dealership. I walked around the showroom inspecting various models. I knew we didn't need a large sedan. I thought about the car I had prayed for earlier. It was just right for our needs. And then, walking down another row of cars, I saw that very car for sale.

I stopped, wondering if I was imagining it. I wanted to be sure. I checked the license plate number—CL 7788. There could be no mistake.

"Sister Reineker," I almost shouted, "this is the car."

The paperwork was soon complete and the sale price fit Sister Reineker's budget perfectly. God's will was accomplished.

Over the years people have asked me how I could pray, "Lord, I claim that car." I'm not one who believes God is some celestial Santa Claus waiting to give us every yacht and mansion on our wish list. (God will supply our needs—not our greeds.) The principle I was operating on is very simple: when I am carrying out the work of God, He will give me whatever is needed to accomplish His work. And, as in the case of the car, the Holy Spirit will make it clear when and how that spiritual authority will be exercised. We must know our need as we actively serve the Lord and we should request the Lord to meet that need.

With only a few exceptions, Susanne and I have not focused our energies on praying for our personal needs. We have spent far more time taking the requests of others to the Lord. But, in turn, God has been faithful to meet our every need.

God certainly promises to supply our needs according to His riches in glory (Philippians 4:19), but that does not suggest each believer will enjoy material wealth. Rather, it means God will not forsake us—we are in His care. For most of us, there will be times when we lack provision. But our reliance on God is strengthened when, in our time of need, we turn to Him for help.

Although we were forced to live on bread, dhall (a lentil) and Marmite spread, while pastoring the church in Kandy, our faith rose to a new level during that period of our lives. God faithfully answered our prayers. What others viewed as hardship and sacrifice, was for Susanne and me actually a season of spiritual preparation for what God had in store for us.

MY ADVENTURE IN FAITH

GLAD TIDINGS TABERNACLE IN KANDY IN THE EARLY
1950'S WHERE COLTON HAD A VISION.

A Question of Eternity

When I look back on our early ministry, I am reminded that our material poverty was nothing compared to the spiritual poverty around us. In Kandy is situated the well-known Buddhist temple in which is enshrined a relic of the Buddha, a single tooth that is revered by worshippers. This temple, the Dalada Maligawa (Temple of the Tooth) has been the venue of many historical ceremonies.

The annual Kandy "perahera" is a series of parades, and is a holy occasion for Buddhists and is a big draw for tourists from around the world. The gold casket containing the tooth relic is borne along the main streets on a richly caparisoned elephant in this resplendent parade. The procession is a spectacular pageant with around 100 elephants, many traditional dancers, and people doing stunts with fire. Thousands of people stream into Kandy. Even throughout the year, that temple is like a magnet to tourists, people seeking meaning to life, and those desiring to venerate the Buddha.

God used these throngs of people to confront me with my lack of compassion to reach out to them with His love. While pastoring and studying for my sermons, I read accounts of the disciples and the acts of the Holy Spirit in the Book of Acts. I concluded there was a great need and we were not meeting it with the same authority exercised by the Early Church. The Holy Spirit gave me a great burden. "Lord," I began to pray, "save our city and touch our nation."

One Sunday as I was dismissing our congregation and shaking their hands at the door as they left, God increased my vision for the lost. Our church families were leaving the sanctuary and walking out into the street. Being few in number, they were quickly lost in the crowds of people out for a Sunday stroll.

I had seen these crowds before. There were faces of local merchants and families that I recognized. But this day was very special. It was as if each passing face caught my eye. I saw the crowd. But I also saw it was composed of individual men and women and young people.

The Holy Spirit spoke to my heart: "What are they doing?"

I felt the emotion rising in my throat. "They are searching for the truth," I said.

But I knew that answer was incomplete. Every day the crowds walked past the church, it was another day they walked farther away from God's love and grace. Each man and woman making that journey with no hope or understanding was ignorant of God's love and His divine judgment. But God, the Divine Judge, is "not willing that any should perish, but that all should come to repentance" (2 Peter 3:9). *He yearns for them to turn to Him and experience His love*, I said to myself.

The Spirit replied to my heart: "They are going into an eternity without Christ. Who will reach them for Me?"

My heart broke. It was as if all of my efforts to share the gospel amounted to nothing. I felt a holy discontent with whatever measure of success my ministry had achieved. What did it matter if our church was filled to capacity with 100 or more believers if tens of thousands were passing us by, totally unaware of God's redemptive love?

An anguish for lost souls gripped me and, for weeks, I could find no peace. I lost my appetite. Sleep was elusive. I prayed at the church. I prayed at home. I prayed as I walked the streets of Kandy.

"God," I pleaded, "show me the way. Don't let one person pass into eternity without knowing of Your love because I was negligent."

I only felt the pain grow sharper. God was not torturing me. He was preparing me to be a soul-winner by letting me experience the pain of a loving Heavenly Father whose children were following a path to destruction.

There was little doubt that some of my priorities were changing. And I was about to embark on the soul-winning adventure of a lifetime.

MY ADVENTURE IN FAITH

COLTON AND
SUSANNE IN THE
EARLY DAYS.

Hand in the Window

In 1956, our eldest son, Chrysantha, was born. Who can fail to be amazed at the miracle of life? But my joy at the new addition to my family was tempered with the growing awareness that millions of boys and girls across Sri Lanka were growing up without an opportunity to hear the message of God's love.

"Lord," I prayed at our little church altar, "You have said there is no other way. You are the only way. There is no other name under heaven whereby people can be saved other than the name of Jesus. You are the only answer. Thousands are going into a Christless eternity. Meanwhile I have the truth of the gospel but I have only about 60 people in my church."

This continued to break my heart. I would weep, then go home. Over the course of the next year I continued to lose my appetite. For days I lost all desire for food. I became distraught. I would cry for no reason. Many times, if someone simply talked to me I would cry. Sleep was now a rarely enjoyed luxury. Susanne, the baby and I would sleep on the same bed. While Susanne and the baby were asleep, I would cry and pray. I did not know what I was praying for, beyond the general anguish I felt for those who were eternally lost. But God was preparing to give me direction with a clarity I never imagined.

It was a typically warm night in 1957. I was seated on the bed facing the window, again unable to sleep. Yet again, I found myself quietly weeping in the dark. Susanne and Chrysantha were deep in their dreams.

The window I faced had small glass panes, one of which was broken. Suddenly, I saw a hand come through that broken pane. I thought it was a burglar. The police had recently warned us about thieves in the area. This was surely a thief trying to reach the window latch on the inside.

I assumed if I were to walk to the light switch and flip it on, the thief would see me and run away. Common sense would say that was actually the best alternative. If the man ran away there would be no confrontation. But I wanted to see that man clearly to give a report to the police.

I slid over the edge of the bed, rolled on the floor until I was near the wall, then switched on the outside light. But there was no one there.

I was puzzled. I knocked off the light, came back to bed and began to pray and cry before God. After a little while, I saw the hand come through the window again. I crept over to the wall and flipped on the inside and outside lights. No one was there.

Turning off the lights, I thought, *What can this be? I have seen this twice now. There is nobody!* Suddenly it dawned on me. *This might be of God.* Quickly, I knelt by my bed and prayed. Within minutes I looked over to the window and saw the hand return.

This time the hand had a glow around it; I knew this was nothing natural. When I saw the nail print in the hand, I gasped. I knew this was my Lord.

I heard a friendly voice. I don't know whether it was from within my mind or aloud in the room, but it was very clear. First, the Lord began to speak to me about my pride and priorities. There were attitudes He wanted to correct in my life.

Suddenly that whole window became like a big screen. I saw crowds of people and many things were being told me, things which I didn't understand completely. Jesus spoke about the crowds and then I saw eight faces that stood out distinctly. He said that in the years to come, I would encounter these people.

Then Jesus spoke to me again about my own life. He lovingly called on me to commit myself to Him.

I was taken aback. Hadn't Susanne and I made every sacrifice in order to minister to our flock of believers in Kandy? Hadn't I agonized for lost souls for the past year and given up my very health as I interceded day and night?

"Lord," I said, "I am committed."

But He was not directing my attention to the past. "Son," He said, "commitment simply means implicit obedience."

I said, "Lord, You know I want to obey You."

There was barely a pause. "Son," the Lord said, "resign your church in a week's time and I want you to go."

I should have said simply, "Yes, Lord." Instead, I said, "Father, You know I have to give one calendar month's notice."

"Where is your commitment?" came the reply.

I accepted His gentle rebuke. "Lord," I said, "I will make the commitment. I will leave."

That was the key impact of that vision on my life. I could have focused on the amazement of such a revelation of the Lord's presence and the sight of Jesus' nail-scarred hand. But the Lord's focus all along was on the foundational point of my relationship with Him. Would I obey without question when I knew that He was leading me?

The Lord began to tell me many other things, but I refrain from sharing those details because some of them have been fulfilled, some are being fulfilled and some are yet to happen. But whenever I speak of that vision on that warm night in 1957 I always speak of the need to unquestioningly obey God. When the believer has that single principle in focus, everything else will fall into place.

"All right, Lord," I repeated, "I will obey, I will go—wherever You lead me."

Destination Colombo

Early in the morning I awoke and gently shook Susanne.
"The Lord met me last night," I said.

She was still half asleep. "What did He say?" she asked.

"Commitment first."

"All right," she said, "what else did He say?"

"No," I replied, "I made a commitment to *God*. You must make a commitment to *me*."

At first, she didn't understand. "Tell me," she persisted.

"No," I said, "you make a commitment and then I will tell you."

Then the meaning of my request dawned on her. "Colton," she said, almost offended, "your God is my God. Where you go I will go. What you do I will do. Your people are my people. Whatever task God gives to you, I will be there."

Mutual commitment has been a very important factor in our life together. Over the years, I have come to understand this in an ever-growing measure. God's Word is so clear. It rightly questions, "Can two walk together, except they be agreed?" (Amos 3:3). As Christ himself promised, "If two of you shall agree on earth as touching any thing that they shall ask, it shall be done for them of my Father which is in heaven" (Matthew 18:19).

In our years of ministry since, I have come to appreciate

the importance of my wife's commitment that day and her agreement to stand with me. Her loving loyalty has kept me moving ahead through times of questioning and discouragement. She has always been a rock of reassurance that we truly could discern the plan and the purpose of God concerning our family and me and the ministry God has given us.

"We are going to leave this church in a week," I said.

"All right," she replied confidently. "If that is what the Lord wants, we will do it."

I handed in my resignation, but the church would not accept it. They had six business meetings trying to convince me to stay. At the final one a dear elderly woman said, "Colton, surely God will change His mind for the sake of these people. Won't you stay with them?"

"I can't," I replied. I knew I had heard from God.

The voice of God comes to you very specifically from the Word and from the Spirit. I certainly believe in the manifestation of the gifts of wisdom and knowledge through other believers. I had all the respect in the world for that dear sister. But my concept of these gifts is that they are often a confirmation of what the Lord has already told you. God is not going to speak to us to act against something He has previously shared with us. The Lord said, "When he, the Spirit of truth, is come, he will guide you into all truth" (John 16:13). Which means the Spirit will unfold the kernel of the truth. He speaks through what we read in God's Word. He speaks further details in the quiet of our hearts. And that teaching is the thing that brings us the conviction that we need to follow through with God's plan for our lives. That plan pierces right through to our heart and we know, "This is what the Lord is telling me," because the Word and the Spirit are actively making that deep impression on our hearts.

Many people ask, "How do you know the voice of God?" I tell them, "My father died more than 50 years ago. If, when he was alive, I had put him in a room with 99 other fathers and told them to call out 'Colton' one at a time, the moment my father called out my name I would know that that was my father." There is no science to this. From the day I was born, I had friendship and fellowship with my father. We talked. And there is something in my ear that picks up his voice. It's the same thing when Jesus says, "My sheep hear my voice . . . and they follow me" (John 10:27). We have to keep talking and walking with God to know His voice.

God had made His voice undeniably clear when He told us to leave the church in Kandy. Colombo was to be our new home. But, like Gideon, it is human nature to keep asking God for a sign even after He has communicated His will. In my case, God used a dramatic miracle while I was still in Kandy to remind me that He truly was sending Susanne and me from the city.

It was our last Sunday night at the Kandy church. After the service, I was asked to visit and pray for a lady who was seriously ill and bedridden. God's plan was to lead me to one of the wealthiest homes in the area. I wondered what God would have me do in such a place. I went to the front door.

Inside was an 84-year-old woman dying of cancer. Doctors had given her only hours to live. Family members were reluctant to let me see the woman. "How can your prayers make a difference," they said, "when the best doctors have accomplished nothing?" They did not want me to disturb her. But I knew God had sent me. Despite their objections, very reluctantly they led me to her side and I prayed.

By the following morning that lady was completely

healed. Even the cataracts in her eyes disappeared. It was as if God had put an exclamation mark on His command for us to follow Him into a new season of ministry. And He allowed that miracle to stand as a lasting testimony among the believers we left behind.

When we left Kandy in 1957, Susanne was within just a few months of giving birth to Eran, our second son. Our family was growing, and we were leaving our humble home to try to find lodging in the capital city. I still had more questions than answers. But I knew God was with me and that He is faithful.

We often become afraid when God tells us to do something with which we're not familiar. But we must obey. We must say, "Lord, show me the way, then I will go and do it." We must be obedient day by day, moment by moment. When we arrived in Colombo (a three-hour journey), for example, we didn't have any place to stay. We didn't know where in the city God wanted us to live; we simply set out in faith. We were unexpectedly invited into the home of a friend to whom I had ministered on earlier occasions. He invited us to stay with him a few days. The Holy Spirit quietly spoke to my heart, "Stay."

During our stay there a missionary from another denomination invited me to accept the pastorate in their church in Galle, with everything provided—house, car and a salary from Sweden. *This is God*, my wife may have thought, but I knew I had a specific calling as the Lord had directed me to Colombo. I had to be still and know that He is God, so I had to say "no" to this excellent offer and wait for God's leading.

Demons and a Prayer

God opened a home for us to hold meetings in. This was after we prayed for a sick child and he was healed. The child's mother asked us to hold a thanksgiving service in her home, which we did. That service led to others, and soon it became a venue for our regular services.

We began to go from place to place holding meetings and staying with friends and relatives. After we had been in Colombo a few months, I felt God wanted Susanne and me to have a place of our own. By that time, Eran, our second son, had joined our family. I prayed about it and asked a Christian lady with experience in real estate to help us.

"Sister," I told her, "I want you to pray with me. God wants me to get a house here and I have to get one."

She smiled, looked a little nervous, then finally spoke. "Very good, Brother Colton, but I want to tell you something. Getting a house in Colombo is like finding a needle in a haystack."

I looked through the window across a sea of houses and commercial buildings. So many buildings, but every one of them housed a tenant. And then God sparked a measure of faith in my spirit.

"Sister," I said with renewed conviction, "don't you know I am the magnet God has sent to extract that needle from the haystack?"

That spark of faith has come to me at so many points in my life. When I meet ministers and fellow believers who are in a quandary as to the next thing they should do, I remind them that we do not go through life aimlessly. As servants of our Heavenly Father we are under divine appointment. We have divine direction and we experience divine fulfillment of God's plan. It is not natural; it is supernatural.

In the days following, God confronted Susanne and me with the supernatural reality of our ministry. I was asked to come and pray for a lady with heart trouble. When I arrived, the husband invited me into his wife's room. I then opened my Bible and felt impressed to begin sharing very earnestly about the power in the name of Jesus. I was doing so as a witness to Christ's healing power.

The woman who complained of heart trouble and appeared to have no energy, jumped from her bed in a rage at the mention of Jesus' name. She had been, in fact, demon possessed.

With her husband's permission and assistance, I took the lady to my sister-in-law's house. Susanne and another minister joined me, and we began to confront the powers of hell that bound that woman's life. One by one, thirty one demons identified themselves and left her as we prayed.

There are many mysteries concerning the spiritual and physical realms. But that night I saw them intersect with undeniable results. The thirty-second and final demon was very resistant and deceptive. We had prayed through the night and were exhausted. Around 8:00 a.m. I demanded that the demon give me a sign he was leaving. He replied that he would break a part of the ceiling and I foolishly consented. When that last demon fled that house of prayer, it shook the ceiling and broke off a large plank that fell to the floor in the room where Chrysantha and my sister-in-law's baby slept. God protected our children. The board fell within inches of their bed.

The demon left, and that woman became one of our most faithful believers. She opened her home to us for prayer services and teaching, and we had many powerful meetings there.

But we still waited for God to supply a place large enough for us to both live and have services. Although our services and opportunities were growing, our financial resources were meager. Every week we would wait for the offering and for God's provision. Susanne had only two saris. I had two sets of clothes. At the gas station I could only afford one half gallon of petrol, but God would stretch that half gallon miraculously. We were often forced to skip meals because we had no money. But still I believed God had spoken to my heart that He would give us a suitable place. We kept praying and believing.

We kept cutting back on our food until one day Susanne said, "What are we going to do now?" We both agreed that we would cut out the babies' milk. Now, that is a hard decision to make. We decided we would give our babies plain tea. In the natural, we knew we were risking malnutrition. But we prayed and put our trust in the Lord.

Like Daniel, who refused King Nebuchadnezzar's rich food and yet grew strong, our sons did not suffer in the least from their diet. My two eldest sons both outgrew me by quite a measure. God's tea was all the nutrition they needed during that season of testing. God's provision is always sufficient for those who trust Him.

MY
ADVENTURE
IN FAITH

COLTON IN AFRICA WITH TRIBAL PEOPLE IN KISII, KENYA.

To Africa

God had stretched our faith when He led us from our church in Kandy to an unspecified ministry in Colombo. Toward the end of 1958, the Lord impressed on my heart that we should launch out in greater faith and press far beyond our own region. I sensed God was calling us to visit Africa.

We did not have the finances for the trip but we did have an invitation from a missionary couple in Africa. So I shared my sense of God's leading with Susanne. As faithful as ever, she heartily agreed to go wherever the Lord was leading. We arranged for the cheapest fare from Colombo to East Africa—Kenya, Uganda and Tanganyika (now Tanzania). Leaving Chrysantha and Eran with my sister Anita, we borrowed some money to pay the fare and started on our journey on July 11, 1959, along with Vincent Abrahams, a man of faith who was a mentor to us.

Our accommodation on the first leg of the journey to Bombay was simple but comfortable. All that changed when we boarded a very small British-India Company boat for the voyage to Mombasa, Kenya's large seaport. Our bunks were in the cargo hold and were nothing more than steel plates attached with chains to the wall. It was open, with no privacy for men and women. Our hearts sank as we realized that we were to travel in these bunks for a week. These bunks were usually used by laborers in

East Africa on the British tea and rubber estates.

I could not allow Susanne to endure this hardship, so I begged for a cabin just for her. But she insisted she would rather stay with me. There was no bedding and we were unable to sleep on the steel plates, so we stored all our suitcases on our bunks and went up to the deck to get some fresh air.

We sat on a bench on the deck and discovered that it was actually more comfortable than the metal bunk in the belly of the boat. So at night Susanne and I slept on that bench under an overcoat. The sea was rough, and the waves sprayed over us.

As the high seas continued we became seasick. Food only made it worse. We were vomiting and had no desire to frequent the dining area. Not wishing to be showered with saltwater a second night, we went in search of another place to spend the night. Ultimately, we found a box about 2 feet wide and 6 feet long where the anchor ropes were stored. This box became our bed each night, as we traveled for about three days with no food. Life felt like an uninterrupted series of nausea attacks and fatigue.

Because of the stormy weather, we were detoured and weighed anchor in Karachi, Pakistan. We were so happy to see land and to no longer feel the deck heaving beneath our feet. We wandered into a hotel and Susanne asked the receptionist if they knew of any Christian church in the area.

"Madame," he replied with some indignation, "this is a strict Islamic country. There are no Christian institutions here."

We decided to take a ride in a tram car. Traveling about the city, we unexpectedly located a church. A group of young people were praying in the church courtyard. They introduced us to their pastor. He and his family fed us and gave us warm, soft beds for the night.

The next morning we expressed our gratitude to the pastor's family. We told them of our missionary journey and the difficult accommodation. They promptly took us to a store and purchased some bedding and fresh fruit for the final leg of our journey.

We set out across the Indian Ocean, sleeping on that same box. It was far from luxurious, but, with the bedding, we were able to manage. We sailed through rising storms and imposing waves. Despite bouts of hunger and seasickness, we finally saw the port of Mombasa as it crept over the horizon. Somehow I knew God was pleased that we had come to Africa. But I still didn't know why He had brought us here.

MY ADVENTURE IN FAITH

COLTON WITH VINCENT ABRAHAMS AND
AKE SODERLUND IN AFRICA.

From Darkness to Light

It was a joy to see Finnish missionaries, Ake and Pirrko Soderlund as we disembarked in Mombasa. Guarded by the ancient Fort Jesus, which had been built by early Portuguese explorers, the town quietly basked in the warm sea breezes off the Indian Ocean. The Christian-named and British-occupied fort, however, coexisted with the region's sizable Muslim community and their mosques.

Within a few hours we had eaten, ensured that our papers were in order and were driving across Kenya in the Soderlunds' Volkswagen. The journey was nearly 500 miles.

We traveled through the day and all night on gravel and unpaved roads as savannah gave way to forest and then to expansive tea plantations near Lake Victoria. We reached Kisii, Kenya, where the Soderlunds lived. From that small town we journeyed into the bush country to share Christ's love with nearby villages.

The Finnish missionaries were opening a new area to the gospel and asked me to teach about 150 people who were training for ministry. I taught a variety of Bible courses through the morning. When we had breaks they used to bring pots of tea that looked like muddy water. Ake was a young missionary with considerable energy and an irrepressible sense of humor. He would sometimes drink their tea but noticed I refused. One day he kept pressing me to have some tea. He made such a show of asking me that I was afraid I might disappoint our village hosts if I refused. I accepted a small cup and managed a few sips with great difficulty. It was so pungent I gulped it down.

"Do you know what you drank just now?" Ake asked with a laugh.

"No," I replied. "What is it?"

"Tea made from a dried grass, and the hot water is mixed with milk, cow's urine and sugar. The cow's urine, they believe, has some medicinal value."

My stomach rolled as I asked for God's grace.

But our differences in culture and diet melted away as I shared God's precious Word with these believers. They worshipped God with abandon.

Their faith knew no bounds. In one service I was exhausted after preaching. There was no time to pray individually with people before the next service. I decided to launch out in faith and pray a mass prayer. I asked the people to lay one hand on the place they had an ailment and lift the other hand to God. I asked the Lord to heal the sick, cast out demons and to meet their needs. I asked them to raise their hands and praise God for the miracles. Then I waited.

I expected to see at least a few people jumping or praising God for miracles they had experienced. Nothing happened.

"How many of you received a miracle after this prayer?" I asked. A few raised their hands so I asked them to share their stories. Their testimonies of healing were powerful. But I confessed that I didn't understand why they were so subdued after God had performed such great miracles for them.

An elderly chief stood, and respectfully spoke through an interpreter:

"There was nothing to shout about. This was what we expected to happen after you prayed. If this did not happen, we would have shouted you down as a fraud. When we ask

God, He gives."

I learned a lesson that day from the very people I thought I had come to teach. Their faith was not based on what they saw—the faith of these believers was based on their unshakeable faith in an invisible God.

We visited another remote village and built a rough platform to attract the people to our services. Tents were set up and with nightfall we lit some kerosene lanterns. African believers beat their drums to announce the service.

The believers sang some African songs and one or two gave their testimonies. Then I was asked to preach.

I had two interpreters. One interpreter translated into Swahili, the national language used among the tribes, and the other into Luo (Dholuo), the local language. As I started preaching on the powerful name of Jesus, I heard screeching, shouting and stampeding beyond the light of our lanterns. Several people in the crowd were possessed by evil spirits and were running around creating turmoil in the service.

"This is dangerous," Ake said. "We should leave at once."

But I felt faith rising in my spirit and I did something I had never done before. I commanded all the demons to stand in line. The power of Jesus' name is so amazing. Where people had been madly running and shaking and shouting, there was soon a line of quiet men and women. We began to pray for them one by one.

A young girl stood at the end of the line. She had approached us earlier in the day when we were building our platform. Though she did not know how to speak a word of English, she had spoken in perfect English saying that we were servants of God and that God was going to use us. I thought of the demon-possessed girl in Philippi when Paul and Silas took the gospel to that ancient city. She had loudly proclaimed that they were messengers from God, but it was only a demonic tactic to bring confusion to their ministry.

Now, as we prayed for the girl standing in line she collapsed in our arms.

The service disbanded and the unconscious girl was taken back to her village. The next day we went to her hut to pray for her again. We noticed that many people had gathered. They wore costumes and masks, and there were also drummers. They were getting ready for the girl's burial as they thought she was dead.

We walked into the little hut in the power of Jesus' name. That girl who was being prepared for burial leaped up and was delivered and set free. Many years later I learned her name was Neri. She had married a Christian minister and they had established a church that grew to some 2,000 people.

In the days that followed we also visited people from the nomadic Maasai tribe. They carried long spears and herded their cattle from place to place. They lived on milk and blood from their animals. Their young warriors recorded the number of people they had killed by tying knots on their spears. These men plaited their hair into long braids and dyed it red.

I didn't remember any dramatic response from the Maasai during our time with them. But, years later, I was at a ministers' conference in East Africa and a well-dressed man in Western clothing approached me.

"Do you remember me?" he asked. "You visited us years ago. I want to tell you that many Maasai pastors are attending this conference. They are serving God and we have many born-again Christians in our tribe. Many of them still remember what you taught them about God during your visit. God used you among us."

At that moment, the Holy Spirit reminded me that we should never become weary in well doing. We must sow faithfully and if we faint not, in due time we will reap a great harvest (Galatians 6:9).

The Voyage Home

We spent about six months ministering among several African tribes. When it was time for us to leave Africa we decided to travel by train from Nairobi, Kenya's capital, to Mombasa to gain passage on a ship home. It was a warm Nairobi afternoon when we boarded the East Africa Railways train. As we left the city behind and headed across the plains, we heard some singing. We walked down the compartment to find a group of people joyfully singing a worship chorus we had heard before. It was a song birthed during a revival that had broken out in Uganda, Kenya's western neighbor. We approached the group and told them we were missionaries. As it was a very long journey, we were able to share God's Word with them and pray with them.

The next day brought us back to Mombasa's humidity and the smell of the sea in the air. We found ourselves on the same ship and, with no more money than when we arrived, sleeping on the same box of anchor ropes all the way to Bombay.

Upon arriving in Bombay, we had no transportation arranged to take us to Sri Lanka. Furthermore no ships were scheduled to make the voyage to Sri Lanka for several weeks. Even though we didn't have any money to pay the bill, we booked a room at the YMCA.

Days passed before we finally convinced a travel agent in Bombay to fly us home on the condition we would pay the balance upon our arrival in Colombo. So, with airline tickets in hand, we returned to the YMCA only to face a different dilemma: we had no money to settle the bill for our room. As we had done time and again throughout our voyage—we prayed. When we asked the manager to tally our bill, we learned that it had already been paid by an evangelist-missionary staying at the YMCA. (One day at breakfast, we saw a fellow believer seated at a table whose poster we had seen before. We had fellowship with him and he told us that he was writing a book and he desperately needed some secretarial work done but was unable to get the assistance he needed. My wife volunteered to help and the work was done. This man, Brother Mattson Boze, had paid our bill, though unaware of our desperate need.)

When God guides, He provides.

Finding the Needle

God had taken us to a remote corner of the world and brought us safely home. But we still needed a permanent residence in Colombo.

The answer to our prayers came unexpectedly when we were asked to visit the home of a couple that had been married for a number of years. Physicians had recently informed them they could not have children.

"God is going to do a miracle," I said to the husband. "Your wife is going to have a baby."

I shared Christ with them and led them in the sinner's prayer.

A short time later, they learned the wife was pregnant. When their beautiful baby girl was born, their excitement knew no bounds.

"What can we do for God?" the mother asked when Susanne and I came to see the baby.

I sensed God was answering our prayers. "Would you let us use this house?" I asked. "Your child cannot go to the prestigious neighboring girls' school for another few years, so would you allow us to use this house until then?"

In any other circumstances, such a request would have seemed audacious. But I knew God was at work. The new parents agreed to my request. They moved to another house and turned over their residence on Walukarama Road to us. This house was in the right location in the heart of the city.

It had a large hall which served as our first church sanctuary. Our third son, Dishan, was added to our family here. All three of our sons were able to gain admission to Royal College, a leading school in Colombo, as living in proximity to the school was a requirement. They were thus able to receive a quality education.

When God asks us to follow through with a specific step of faith, then we must obey. Confessing everything that comes into our heads or endeavoring to use mind-over-matter techniques doesn't accomplish anything. Too many people try that approach and then become despondent when they don't receive what they confessed. There has to be an uncompromising conviction that, most of all, we want God's perfect will when we seek His provision. That is why we need to know the voice of God. John 10:27 says, "My sheep hear my voice . . . and they follow me." It is not because someone says, "Believe and you will prosper." We believe in God's adequate provision, but every individual has to personally hear the voice of God and seek to do His will.

God's leading gives structure to our faith and gives us guidance in how He desires to bless us. James explains this interaction and shows how fruitless it is to pray for "blessings" that are, in reality, outside the will of God. James 4:2,3 says, "Ye have not, because ye ask not. Ye ask, and receive not, because ye ask amiss, that ye may consume it upon your lusts." James explains why some people do not enjoy God's blessing—they are not in communion with God. They bombard heaven with requests for more of the world's possessions, yet their hearts are not hungry for more of Jesus. As we listen to the voice of the Holy Spirit, as we strive to carry out God's purpose for our lives and to serve others in love, we will discern the true blessings God has in store for us. When that discernment combines with faith, we can rest assured that our prayers will be answered.

The Gospel Opposed

Sharing the truth of Christ is never without challenges and opposition. Our Lord himself said the world would despise us just as it hated Him (John 15:18). The world that Christ has called us to reach with His message of love will find a thousand ways to oppose that message.

I remember an instance early in my ministry when I had finished Bible school and was pastoring in Makevita at my father's church. I was also holding street meetings and ministering in the villages. Despite the move of God in these services, some people still opposed me.

One day I went to a nearby village to hold a service. I knew it would be a small crowd. The rains had come and it was flooding. The road was practically impassable in places. I was traveling with two older men and three older women from my church. I discovered that the hymn books had been forgotten. So I hiked back through the mud and the flooded portions of the road to get them. I waded through water holding the hymnals high above my head. As I stepped back onto the road, a gang of drunks blocked my path.

"Where do you think you're going?" one asked with an angry slur.

They knew very well where I was going. They had no intention of letting me continue my journey. The others circled and grabbed me, knocking the hymnals to the ground. One pulled a grubby and stained handkerchief from his pocket and tied it over my eyes. Then the beating began. Paul the apostle wrote of being whipped, stoned and beaten with rods. These men preferred their fists and feet. Then they got creative and grabbed me by the ankles and began to drag me through the deep mud.

The gang leader retrieved my Bible from the road and handed it to me.

"We'll let you go," he said. "All you have to do is tear up that cursed book and renounce this 'Christ' whose lies you keep spreading."

There was a day when, despite my small stature, I would have fought these men with my last ounce of strength. But that Colton had been overwhelmed by the love of the Savior they wanted me to renounce—the Jesus who had meekly laid down His life on a cross so these same drunks could be saved.

I said, "If I forsake Christ, I'm dead. I have no life."

So they beat me some more, and I knew by the strength of their blows they truly intended to end my life.

"Wait," I called out. They stopped, wondering if I was about to comply with their demands. "Wait," I repeated. "A man condemned to the gallows still gets a last request."

"What do you want?" the leader asked.

"I must pray," I said. And to their great surprise, I knelt in the muddy water and prayed out the entire sermon I had prepared to preach in the village. They beat me up some more and threatened to kill me, but I could tell that the message of the gospel had unnerved them. God promises that His Word will absolutely never fail to have its intended result (Isaiah 55:11).

I was unmarried and I had my mother's address. I took

it from my Bible and gave it to them. I instructed them that if I had to go through a watery grave they should drop my mother a postcard and tell her I would meet her in heaven. I then told them, "Water can't kill me, fire can't burn me, until God wants me."

Suddenly, in a last desperate surge of anger, they threw me into the river. I was badly beaten up, but I felt the Lord's strength. One of the men held on to my hand and said, "Don't kill him." I pulled myself back to the surface. When my head came out of the water, I was preaching.

The men left me. I proceeded to the meeting and preached as scheduled. I knew that day that I had stared death itself in the face. By a strange coincidence, the leader of that gang drowned at that same spot the following week.

Some years later, after we had started the work in Colombo, as we had no baptism tank, we took some people to that same river in the village to baptize them. When the ladies found it difficult to get in, a man from the village who was standing by jumped in to assist them. When I looked at his face, I saw it was the same man who had held my hand to save me.

While at Walukarama Road in 1961, Susanne and I regularly visited the sick and needy. We never worried about our safety or imagined any dangerous situations that we might encounter. One afternoon while I was preparing for a typical round of visits, a man rushed into our house to announce an urgent need. He insisted that we both come to pray for someone.

My sister was living with us, and Susanne said to her, "Please take care of the children. We are going on this journey, and we do not know what time we will be back."

There was something about the invitation from this man that troubled my spirit. I was growing more disturbed by the minute. I felt the Holy Spirit prompting me, and I went outside and walked up to the taxi driver who had driven the man to our house.

"From where did this man hire this taxi," I demanded, "and where did he say he was taking us?"

The driver was bewildered at my abrupt question, but gave me the destination.

The Spirit of God then revealed to me that this was a plan by some godless men to harm us and thwart our ministry. They were going to take us to a remote place. They planned to push me out of the car and take Susanne away. The entire plot was clearly revealed to me by the Spirit, as if the stranger had suddenly admitted it himself.

I returned to the house and told the stranger in no uncertain terms we were not accompanying him and he was to leave our home. A look of terror swept across his face and he hastily retreated to the taxi.

God saved us from a treacherous situation. We could have fallen prey to that snare and quite possibly never seen our family again. But God is faithful; He is never late and never early. He is there on time to deliver His people who have committed their very lives to Him.

CHAPTER 27

God's House—a Horse Stable

We held meetings in the house on Walukarama Road for four years. In 1964, with their daughter now old enough to attend school, the owners needed to move back into their house. So Susanne and I looked for another location and found a small house to rent on Deanstone Place, which was also in Colombo.

Where our previous home had been spacious, this one was quite cramped. The people attending our services had to find creative ways to seat themselves. Many had to stand during the entire meeting. But God was in our midst, bringing in His joy and power.

We continued for two years with the services at Deanstone Place. Then, in 1966, Asoka and Elfie Corea, who had been touched when Asoka's sister was healed of a chronic stomach ailment some years before, approached me with an offer.

"Pastor Colton," they said, "we have some abandoned horse stables on our property that you may be able to use for holding services if they were remodeled."

I visited their home, saw the stables, and was thrilled at the opportunity to grow and establish our congregation. We simply broke down all the stall divisions and created one open space. After a couple of months of remodeling, we held a dedication service.

"Surely, if Christ is pleased to have the world celebrate His birth in a manger, He has nothing against His followers gathering to worship Him in stables," I told Susanne.

By moving to the larger building, our congregation took on additional stability. And, as word of the converted horse stables circulated, many others joined the congregation. God can truly establish His church in any setting as long as the presence of the Holy Spirit is evident.

With the church's move to the stables, our quarters at Deanstone Place were no longer so cramped. After nine years we were now able to have our home separate from the church.

Yet again, God had proved His faithfulness to our family and to our ministry. It was 1966 and we found ourselves in an established parsonage with a growing congregation in a unique, but equally established, church building. Little did I know that God was about to test my faith by pulling out from under me everything that brought me security.

One Step at a Time

Son, God spoke clearly to my heart in 1967, *it is time for you to make a trip around the world.*

Like Sarah, to whom the Lord promised a son in her old age, I was incredulous. "Lord, travel around the world?" By this time, I no longer had a car. Our finances had simply grown too tight. I was getting by with a small motorcycle. Traveling across Colombo was enough of a challenge. Now was God really telling me I was going to travel internationally?

Susanne and I had a very simple agreement. "You trust God," she would say, "and I will trust you for our daily needs."

"God," I prayed, "if I am to go around the world, how can my wife take care of three children?" I waited for God to see the logic of this objection and let me off the hook.

Divine silence.

"Lord," I prayed with resignation, "if You want me to, I will do it."

I sold my motorcycle. It was the only option I saw for securing the funds necessary to travel. But I knew it would barely begin to pay for the trip.

A businessman said, "Brother Colton, I heard you have some money from your motorcycle. Let me invest it and double the money for you." I did not consult God and quickly gave the money to this man. After two weeks, he returned—not with a check, but with a sincere apology:

"Oh, Brother Colton, I lost your money, I lost my money and I lost the business."

"Oh, God," I prayed, "why did You allow this? That was all I possessed. I have lost everything."

If I had thought it through, I would have realized I had no reason to blame God for my loss. Had I consulted Him in the first place, I would have been justified in questioning Him about it. But I had acted on my own. We often do the thing we want to do and then shift the responsibility to God. That is where I made the mistake. A man offered a plan and I jumped at it because I assumed it was God's way of meeting the financial need. But God's way, God's will and God's plans are all accomplished through *His* means. We must be discerning and be obedient to the will, the plan and the purpose of God.

So there I was sitting in my little home and rubbing my hands and blaming God. "Father," I kept praying, "why did You allow this to happen? That's the only possession I had, and You allowed me to sell it and allowed me to give the money to this man and I have lost it all."

My prayers took on a rebellious spirit. "Father," I found myself praying, "You're not getting me to travel anywhere. I'm not going at all. I'm not going to make any trips for You."

I had reached a spiritual valley. The old Colton was rearing his ugly head. But in the midst of my angry prayers, a car came and parked outside my home. I looked out the window and was surprised to see a lady I knew coming to the door. She was a teacher of oriental dancing in the local schools and she belonged to the Anglican Church. She used to come and take me to pray for the sick. She was the last person I wanted to see. But when you are a minister, you can't carry your feelings on your sleeve. And I wasn't about to reveal to her my less-than-stellar attitude toward God. I quickly buried my unholy anger, put on a great big smile and answered the door.

"Sister," I said, "come in."

In Sri Lanka, a country where tea is plentiful, we say, "Any time is tea time." When visitors come to your home, you invite them to take a seat and you offer them tea. While you sip tea you discuss your business. Instead of a teapot boiling, however, I was the one boiling inside.

The woman entered and remained standing when I invited her to take a seat. There was an awkward silence. She looked at me. I peered back awkwardly. My smile was beginning to waver as I thought of the unfinished business I had with God.

"Sister," I asked, trying not to show my agitation, "do you want me to go and pray for somebody?"

"No," she replied softly.

I stood a moment longer, waiting for her to explain her visit. "Sister," I prodded, "do you want me to pray for you?"

"No, I don't need prayer."

More uncomfortable silence.

Finally, I could stand it no longer. "What do you want?" I asked bluntly.

She just looked at me, and when I was about to explode in exasperation she spoke with a nervous waver in her voice. "How can I tell a man of God like you that God spoke to me about you?"

I was speechless. I could have accepted a word from God through a spiritual leader or at least a Pentecostal. But she was an Anglican dance teacher. My spiritual pride assumed those were the rules. But God brought to my mind all the bitter prayers I had thrown in His face. I had been in no condition to hear from Him. He had sent this humble sister to break through my belligerence.

"Sister," I said, "if God really spoke to you and gave you a message, then I need to hear His word for me."

"This has never happened to me," she said earnestly. "I was just sweeping my bedroom when I heard a voice. It only said, 'Go and tell Pastor Colton that I will show him one step at a time.' I don't know what that means, but I knew I must relay this message to you."

"That's just what I need to hear," I practically shouted. She was surprised at my response, but obviously relieved that I understood the message she had obediently conveyed.

She returned to her car, and I returned to my knees, humbled at the faithfulness of God.

"Lord," I prayed, "I'm very sorry. I will go. I will surely go for You and I will be what You want me to be."

I still didn't have any money. But that no longer mattered. I had to prepare for the journey that was at hand.

Bound for Bombay

I wondered how Susanne would react to my proposal to travel alone and leave her with the children. But, as always, she was a tower of strength and faith.

"If you can trust God to go around the world without money," she said with a smile, "I will trust God for the three boys and myself."

It wasn't long before the Anglican friend paid us another visit. This time she revealed that God had spoken to her to help care for my wife and children while I was away. Again, I was struck by God's choice of this lady. He looked past the small group of people to whom we ministered and brought this sister from across the wider body of Christ to be a mother to my wife.

Over the next few weeks, one miracle after another brought in the equivalent of $500 for my airline ticket.

At this time in Sri Lanka, a new government had come into power that prohibited ordinary citizens from leaving the country. Nevertheless, I made my travel request known to the immigration authorities.

"No Sri Lankans can travel abroad," the officer told me bluntly.

With a firm conviction that God was planning this trip, I didn't back down. I told the man I had to go abroad and I would be back to press my request.

Two weeks later I returned and discovered that the law had been changed. The new guidelines allowed a Sri

Lankan to travel abroad once in a lifetime on a spiritual or cultural pilgrimage. If I were a Hindu or a Buddhist I could go to India. If I were a Roman Catholic, I could go to Rome. Being a Protestant, I could go to Jerusalem.

The law allowed me to buy a ticket from Sri Lanka to Jerusalem and a return ticket home. I could spend a maximum of $500 on the pilgrimage. "That's just enough," I told the man.

I would first go to Bombay where my ticket would be rerouted to Jerusalem. My $500 was converted into travelers' checks and stamped "Only to be cashed in Jerusalem." I had no money; I had a ticket to Bombay, and from there I had an open ticket to reroute to Jerusalem.

It was a March day when Susanne and the three boys accompanied me to the airport. We were excited about this new adventure in faith. We kissed each other goodbye and I boarded the plane for Bombay.

But when I took my seat and looked from the little window, I spotted my wife and three small children. They looked so alone, so helpless. Suddenly, every fearful thought I had suppressed took hold of my spirit. *What am I doing? Where am I going? I have not made any provision for them. They don't have any income. I don't have tickets to go around the world. I don't have the money. I don't have any friends waiting for me.*

Fear gripped me and I began to cry. "Dear Lord," I prayed through my tears, "what am I doing?"

The plane took off. I put my head in my hands, my shoulders shaking with emotion. "Lord," I prayed in desperation, "I will not ask You again—only this once. Please, Lord, confirm to me that I am in Your will. Please send an angel to this plane and confirm to me that I am going in the center of Your will."

As I was praying, I felt a gentle touch on my hand. I

thought the angel of the Lord truly had boarded that plane. When I opened my eyes, however, I did not see an angel but a somewhat distraught airhostess.

"Are you sick?" she asked.

"No, no," I said hastily, hoping she hadn't seen my tears. "I'm fine."

"Do you want a bag in case you become nauseous?" she persisted.

"No," I replied, "I don't need anything."

But she would not leave me alone. "The pilot would not want me to leave you in this condition," she said. Before I could object, she sat next to me. Over the next hour, through her simple conversation, God used her to brighten my outlook on life. My anticipation for what God had in store for me returned.

That old Dakota plane lumbered through the clouds as fast as its ancient rivets would allow. We landed an hour or two late in Bombay. But little did I know that many months would pass before I would set foot again in my homeland. I was embarking on the journey of a lifetime.

MY ADVENTURE IN FAITH

THE COLTON WICKRAMARATNE FAMILY IN 1967.

'God, I Need Help'

It was dusk when the small plane arrived in Bombay. After disembarking, I was given a ride downtown to the airline office. I yanked on the front door—but to no avail. The office was closed and I had no other place to get my ticket rerouted to Jerusalem.

What could I do? I had no friends, no money, no place to go and early the following morning the flight departed for Jerusalem.

"God," I prayed, "I need help. Your Word promises that where two or three are in agreement You will answer their prayer." I placed one hand over the other. "I have no one to agree with, so I am in agreement with You and I believe You can get me to the place You want me to go."

I began to praise God in advance for the answer to my prayer. I opened my eyes. At the corner of the building a small door opened and a man with a briefcase walked out. Immediately God spoke to my heart with the same clear voice that I had heard 10 years before when I saw the vision of the Lord's hand.

He is the man.

I ran up to the stranger. "Sir, Sir," I called, trying to get his attention without alarming him. He stopped and eyed me with suspicion. "I come from Sri Lanka," I explained, "and I have to get my ticket rerouted." I pulled my ticket out and gave it to him. "I have to have the ticket rerouted so I can go to Jerusalem."

He casually glanced at the tickets. "Yes," he agreed, "we have to reroute these. The office is closed until 9 o'clock tomorrow. Come back then, and we will serve you first and get you on your way."

He returned my tickets and began to walk away.

"Father," I prayed, "now what am I going to do?"

The clear, guiding voice replied, *He is the man.*

I ran after the man. "Sir, Sir, I have no place in Bombay to stay the night."

He was getting impatient, but he stopped and pointed up the street. "You see that hotel over there?" he asked. "It's a cheap place, but it's a clean place. You can stay the night over there."

Father, now what am I going to do? I prayed silently. The reply was not urgent, but direct: *He is the man.*

I ran to the man again. "Sir, I don't have any money to stay in the hotel."

"That's not my problem," he said, turning to walk away. He climbed into his car.

"Father, now what am I going to do?" I prayed in desperation.

Again the still, small voice said: *He is the man.*

Without thinking I ran around the car, jumped into the passenger's side and closed the door. The man glared at me in shock and anger. His face burned red and he began to yell at me as if I were about to rob him. He drew back his fist.

"Sir," I said, raising my finger to his face, "you don't know who you're talking to."

He looked at me with growing perplexity. "What did you say?"

"You don't know who you're talking to," I repeated.

"Well, who are you?" he asked.

"You should have asked that question a long time ago,"

I replied. "I am no ordinary traveler. I am on a special errand for my Father."

Under the Spirit's leading, I shared my story of how God spoke to me, how I left my wife and three children in God's hands and how I was making this trip in obedience to my Heavenly Father.

"If you help me," I concluded, "God is going to bless you. If you don't help me, I'll leave you in the hands of the Lord." I turned and began to open the door.

"Wait, wait," he said, "don't do that."

He got out of his car, picked my suitcase off the sidewalk and walked back to his office. Inviting me inside, he took my ticket and rerouted it. Then he invited me back to his car. Placing my suitcase in his trunk, he drove me to one of the nicest hotels in Bombay, the Taj Mahal.

He went to the receptionist and gave her his business card. "Give this gentleman a first-class air-conditioned room," he said, "and give him a tour of Bombay by night. Charge it to our account."

Once again God confirmed He was my tour guide. He would show me where to go, what to say, and whom to meet. My duty was to simply obey.

MY
ADVENTURE
IN FAITH

THE FIRST WORLD ASSEMBLIES OF GOD COMMITTEE.

New York City

Arriving in Jerusalem, I met another couple from Sri Lanka, a Christian minister and his wife. They had arranged a tour and they invited me to join them at their expense. The gentleman had been to Jerusalem before and he served as my guide. So I enjoyed their company for 10 days and I still had my $500. Thanks to their generosity, I was able to see the Holy Land.

After the tour, I went to a travel agent in Jerusalem and gave him the $500 and my return ticket to Sri Lanka. "Sir," I explained, "take this return ticket and the $500 and fly me towards the United States as far as possible."

The man looked at the ticket and the money. "I'm very sorry," he said, "I can only send you to Sri Lanka. I have other customers. Sorry I can't help you."

I stood in line again. When I reached his desk, he glared back at me with steely eyes. "Stay here—I'll be back."

It was a long process as he worked on my tickets between serving other customers. I spent time in the waiting area, reading and pacing. Finally, that afternoon he called me back to his desk. Without smiling, he said, "Your $500 and the value of the air tickets back to Sri Lanka are enough to get you to Kennedy Airport in New York."

I thanked him, but he didn't respond. To him I was just another customer. He didn't know he was part of a miracle.

Hours later I boarded a plane for New York City.

At Kennedy International Airport, planes were landing and taking off in a constant roar as I went to retrieve my baggage. I collected my suitcase and found a seat in the waiting area. God had taken me to Bombay and Jerusalem one step at a time. Now I was on the other side of the world. But I did not have one cent in my pocket. My fears resurfaced. So again I placed my hand over my other hand and said, "Lord, one more miracle and I'll be out of this predicament too. Please help me; I don't want to stay here and it's getting late. You have to do something for me." Again, I began to thank Him for the answer.

That's the only day in America that I liked having a long name. If I were called Smith, Jones or some other name, I would have missed my cue. Suddenly I heard an American trying to pronounce my name over the public address system.

I ran to the counter. "Sir," I said, "you're calling for Colton Wickramaratne from Sri Lanka."

"No," the ticket agent said, "we're calling for a minister."

"I am a minister—Colton Wickramaratne from Sri Lanka!"

Then he said, "This lady wants to see you."

I looked at the woman standing at the counter. We had never seen each other before. She pulled something from her handbag. In amazement, I saw Susanne's handwriting.

A few years before, a woman from the United States had visited Sri Lanka. She belonged to the Lutheran church and had heard me preach at a camp meeting. When I invited people who wanted to receive the baptism in the Holy Spirit to come forward, she responded to the altar call.

"Pastor and Mrs. Wickramaratne, if you ever come to America," she later wrote, "please visit my home."

Susanne had found the woman's letter and written to her after I had informed Susanne that my travel plans to the U.S.A. were finalized: "My husband is arriving in the States," she had said. "If you want to meet him, please go to Kennedy Airport in New York because I don't know his program."

The woman had asked one of the members of her prayer group to meet me at the airport and bring me to her home.

"She told me you were a busy man," the woman from the prayer group said, "but she wanted me to ask you to cancel your engagements and come with me to her home. She is currently out of town but will return from her trip shortly."

I gladly accepted the invitation. I was taken to a car and they drove me to an exclusive community in New York, where we entered a beautiful apartment complex.

In my host's apartment, I found a letter waiting for me. I opened it and found $25 for my incidental expenses. The letter listed a number where I could call for a car. I was also told the refrigerator was full of food and every morning one of the ladies from the prayer group would come and make me a hot meal. I was to consider the apartment my home away from home.

"Well, if you are going to come and make me a hot meal," I told the lady who had given me a ride, "I'll give you and your friends a Bible study every morning."

She nodded her head. "That's a deal."

At the time, however, I had no comprehension of the victories and challenges that would come from that Bible study.

MY ADVENTURE IN FAITH

COLTON AND SUSANNE WITH THEIR DAUGHTER, ROSHIE.

God's Fool

The Bible studies were blessed times that encouraged
me as much as the ladies who attended. One asked me to
share with her husband some of my faith experiences. Her
husband was an attorney working in New York.

He accompanied her one day to the Bible study.
The three of us sat together and I told him about my
conversion, about the wonderful way the Lord led me to
Bible school, about the calling of God on my life and how
the Lord gave me prophecies and visions that had led me
around the world.

It was an intimate setting, and I began to sense that this
man needed to hear my story. I held nothing back and
shared each testimony in great detail, thinking he would
gain a better understanding of God's desire to work in our
lives.

I told the attorney of God's provision in Bombay and
Jerusalem, and even how I arrived in New York. As I
spoke, I was reminded again how marvelous and amazing
God's tremendous provision had been. "God cares. God
loves and understands. And God holds the blueprint of
our lives in His hands," I said. "If we put our trust in
Him, He will never fail us, He will never leave us, He will
never forsake us, He will carry us through."

I waited for his response. I fully expected the man to
accept Christ as his personal Savior and Lord. I thought
he would see the Scriptures as truth.

He sat across from me for a minute, staring. He examined me from head to toe. Then he spoke thoughtfully. "You know," he said, "if I've ever met a fool, the biggest fool I've met is you."

I was as shocked as I was offended. He continued, "If I were you, I would beg, borrow or steal and do everything possible to return to my wife and children. Your responsibility is them."

His wife sat next to him greatly embarrassed. He plowed on. "It's a very foolish assumption to think that God is guiding, that God is providing. These are nothing but coincidences that have happened in your life. You can't take these kinds of chances and leave your wife and children at the mercy of circumstances."

He and his wife made an awkward exit and I was left alone to ponder his remarks in the luxury apartment that God had provided for me "by coincidence."

"God," I prayed, "I'm Your child, I'm Your servant, and this man is calling me a fool."

The same Jesus who issued the Great Commission to His followers and told them to take the gospel into all the world also warned about casting pearls before swine "lest they trample them under their feet, and turn again and rend you" (Matthew 7:6). There are people who not only refuse to accept God's truth, but will brazenly attack those whom God sends to share it. I learned that it takes wisdom to discern the true opportunities for proclaiming the precious truths God had made so clear to my heart.

The attorney's verbal assault and his inability to understand faith served as an illustration of 1 Corinthians 2:14: "The natural man receiveth not the things of the Spirit of God: for they are foolishness unto him: neither can he know them, because they are spiritually discerned."

From that day on, if anyone would ask me, "Colton,

what are you doing? Where are you going? What is your business?" I would tell them quite confidently, "You know, my Father owns the biggest insurance company in the world and I am traveling for Him. I am also canvassing policies for my Father's insurance company."

This statement is the truth: My Heavenly Father owns the cattle on a thousand hills (Psalm 50:10); the silver and the gold are His (Haggai 2:8). He is the Creator of the earth and the entire universe (Genesis 1:1). Also, my Father has prepared a heaven, a place to keep people from the everlasting fire prepared for the devil and his angels (Matthew 25:41). Therefore, I am in the business of canvassing policies and insuring people and giving them that eternal security found only in the Lord Jesus Christ.

MY ADVENTURE IN FAITH

RICK SEAWARD (SECOND FROM LEFT), CHIEF GUEST AT THE NARAHENPITA NEW CHURCH BUILDING DEDICATION.

Miss Greer

The ladies in our Bible study continued to grow more enthusiastic about the truths we were sharing. "Brother Colton," they said, "you must meet our ministers. They don't believe in God."

I was amazed. Ministers who did not believe in God? "Of course," I said, "I need to meet them."

We set a date and time, and I prepared to serve them plenty of Sri Lankan-style tea. Five ministers came that day and I told them my entire story. One of them served as spokesman for the group. He sounded like the attorney who had ridiculed me.

"Brother Colton, the missionaries have brainwashed you thoroughly. We don't contact God in the ways you describe. We certainly don't talk about Jesus' blood or anyone else's blood. It makes Christianity a bloody religion. Today, people have miracles without going through Jesus."

I was taken aback. This was my introduction to the supposedly Christian nation of the United States.

"We'll prove to you what we say," the "minister" continued. "Would you like to meet a woman who contacts God without going through Christ, without calling up worn-out ideas like sacrifice and blood?"

"Yes, I would like to meet her," I said firmly. "But know right now, I don't believe contacting God in this manner is possible."

We arranged a date for a meeting with this woman (whom I will call Miss Greer), the five "ministers," and the women of our Bible study. We all sat down to tea.

The man who had denounced me during our previous meeting said to Miss Greer, "This man has been brainwashed. Tell him how you contact God."

She began to talk to me in a very condescending manner. She presented herself as one who embodied supreme truth. But instantly I knew she was nothing more than a practitioner of the occult and witchcraft.

The occult and witchcraft are common in Sri Lanka. But she was fumbling and mumbling away as if she had stumbled onto some new spiritual reality and that it was our privilege to have her share it with us. She had "Reverend" in front of her name, and she had earned some kind of counterfeit theological doctorate. So she had a way of twisting and mingling high-sounding theology with the lies of hell.

"Miss Greer," I said, "would you kindly keep it simple."

The ministers, who had sat in rapt attention during her spiel, laughed heartily at that remark. "This man is a simpleton," they said. "The missionaries have got him mixed up. Go ahead and tell it to him simply."

"Let's get right to the point," I said. "When you want to see the miraculous, what methods are you using? When I pray for people in need, I lay hands on them in faith; I anoint them with oil in obedience to the Scriptures. Whatever God leads me to do, I obey and people are healed. How do you do it?"

Miss Greer's eye's flashed. When she spoke, it was with a sarcastic laugh. "All right, all right," she said. "I'll tell you. Sometimes I smile it out. Sometimes I feel it out. Sometimes I laugh it out. Sometimes . . ."

She was seated across from me. She was the center of

attention. The women in our Bible study and the ministers were swallowing every word.

Suddenly, I felt the Holy Spirit become grieved, and anger swelled within me. I forgot I was in the great city of New York. Had I closed my eyes and listened to her tirade, I would have been convinced I was back in Sri Lanka. Through the years, I had encountered other people filled with evil spirits. *Here is a woman,* I thought, *with the spirit of divination.*

I could no longer contain myself. I leaped from my chair toward her. I reached out and grabbed the woman by the hair—as I had done in Sri Lanka when I confronted those possessed by demons. It turned out to be a wig. It came off her head and everyone gasped. I too was shocked, as until that day I did not know that women wore hairpieces. But I hardly heard the angry protests of the ministers, because my focus was on confronting the demonic spirit controlling her.

I dropped the wig and grabbed Miss Greer by the neck. I was not fighting *her,* but rather confronting the evil spirit. I didn't stop to think I was in America and this kind of behavior wasn't permitted. I was simply following the Holy Spirit.

"You foul demon," I commanded, "come out of her in Jesus' name."

The moment I said that she fell to the floor writhing and frothing from her mouth. I got down on my knees next to her and prayed with authority. The battle raged several minutes. Then the room grew silent.

"You've assaulted a woman in New York," the ministers threatened. "We all saw it. You can be put in prison."

But then they witnessed the demons coming out of her and fear swept across their faces.

I went to the refrigerator and took a bottle of cold water

and splashed it on Miss Greer's face.

"You need to know the Lord," I said.

"Yes," she said tearfully.

I led her in the sinner's prayer and she opened herself to Jesus. She accepted Christ.

"You know nothing," she said to the ministers. "The Lord has sent this man."

Then she turned to me and told us her story. She was a registered nurse in New York. She led a promiscuous life, and had many men who would do anything for her.

"There was one man in my life that I couldn't give up," she said. "One day when I was working in the hospital, the ambulances brought in several people from a terrible accident. The doctors were fighting for their lives when I passed the trauma room."

She heard the doctors comment about one of the accident victims. "Nothing can be done," they said. She turned to see the patient they were discussing and recognized it was the man she loved.

"I got so desperate and so helpless when I saw him," Miss Greer said. "I began to cry hysterically because I knew he was dying. Then I raised my hands standing next to his stretcher. I said, "If there is any power in the universe that can help me save him, then I will give my life to that power.'"

Suddenly, she said, it felt as if electricity coursed through her hand and entered her body. An insidious voice whispered in her mind: *Feel him and he will live.*

She obeyed. She felt the same power move through her hand into the man. He recovered, and from that day she knew she possessed some strange spiritual power. It is dangerous when you are living a sinful life to seek spiritual power, as you open yourself to the control of demons.

God delivered Miss Greer that day. He also opened my

eyes to the deceitful practices of "the god of this world" who blinds the minds "of them which believe not, lest the light of the glorious gospel of Christ, who is the image of God, should shine unto them" (2 Corinthians 4:4). I had seen such satanic tactics in my homeland. I now recognized the prince of darkness to be equally active in the West. But I would soon encounter even more compelling evidence.

MY
ADVENTURE
IN FAITH

COLTON ADDRESSING THE DELEGATES AT IMPETUS '86.

Hell's Cathedral

After I exposed Miss Greer's demonic deceptions, I thought the group of ministers would never come to see me again. They weren't exactly thrilled with losing their mentor. But they arrived one afternoon waving a paper in my face.

"Colton," they said triumphantly, "read this!"

I read the bold headline: "An Evening With God."

"Since you are so sold out to God and you like communing with Him," one of them said, "we thought we'd take you to this meeting."

Now, from the wording on the flyer, I decided it must be some charismatic or Pentecostal meeting. Who else would advertise so boldly about spending an evening with God?

"I'm delighted that you want to take me," I said.

As we approached the large auditorium, I saw crowds of young people. I was shocked. "It's wonderful to see so many young people going to church," I told the ministers. "We might not get a seat."

"Don't worry, we already bought tickets," they said.

I didn't want to say anything, but I was thinking, *These crazy Americans buy tickets to go to church?*

We made our way through the crowds to our seats. I began to take in the surroundings and realized this was no ordinary church service. For one thing, beams of colored light were weaving into each other all over the building. My group of hosts sat on either side of me. Suddenly, when the lights were dimmed, I felt the men next to me take a good grip on my arms.

The curtain at the front opened and a young black man with a guitar came on stage and began to sing. The moment he opened his mouth, I knew my hosts had misled me. The guitarist began to sing the filthiest lyrics. I knew the ministers expected me to react, so I kept my face emotionless.

After the guitarist was finished, a young man came forward to give a "testimony." He turned out to be a blaspheming comedian. He began to ridicule Christianity in a way that had the entire audience laughing.

"I was passing a church," he said, "and I saw on the bulletin board 'Jesus is the Answer.' Now, what I want to know is, 'What's the question?'"

The people were rolling with laughter by now.

Another person came forward and began to talk about the joys of his evil lifestyle. After that another person delivered a graphic monologue on sex.

"Ladies and gentlemen, you must excuse me," he said. "What I'm going to read is pretty hard-core, but I'm compelled to read it."

As he began to read, I recognized the piece to be from the sacred writings of the Song of Solomon describing the bride. But as he read, he constantly interrupted himself to give a vulgar, filthy interpretation of the verse.

"You know where this filth comes from?" he asked. I could almost see him winking. "It's from the Bible!" The crowd went wild.

My blood was boiling, but I showed no reaction that would give my hosts ungodly satisfaction.

Someone claiming to be a preacher came next. He had three points in his "sermon": (1) You pray and do everything you can to contact God, but you can't reach

Him. (2) It turns out that you can't awaken God. He's been experimenting with psychedelic drugs. He's in a coma and there's no way to revive Him. (3) You finally realize (and at this point the man produced a newspaper to read from) that God is dead and buried and His obituary has been printed.

In my country, I thought, *even those who claim to be atheists wouldn't do a thing like this.*

When the "preacher" was finished with his harangue against God, another man appeared. He wore an Eastern robe and sat cross-legged like the yogis. He began to chant. In a long, wailing tune he said many things that sounded good at first. He spoke of God creating the earth and speaking to man in the cool of the evening. He told how God spoke through the prophets and then sent His Son the Lord Jesus Christ. He even spoke of sacred Communion and explained that the bread represents the body of Christ and the wine represents His blood.

Where is he going with this? I wondered. I didn't have to wait long to find out. In an instant the man threw up his arms and shouted, "Praise God! God has done away with all those rituals and God has brought in a new emblem into the church today to reveal himself in a more realistic manner to mankind. He has given us today a new ritual, a new communion, and that communion is LSD!"

By that time, they were distributing the drug in the hall.

Then the curtain fell for intermission. My hosts were smiling, laughing and having a good time. They released my hands and stood to go buy food at a concession stand.

Under the direction of the Holy Spirit, I ran toward the stage. The ministers chased me down the aisle, up the stairs to the stage and through the curtain. There I found the man who administered the "communion" and all his cronies seated at a long table drinking beer.

I shook my fist. "Sir," I shouted with the Spirit's authority, "you have deceived these people. You said there is no God. I spoke to Him just minutes ago. You have a prince of demons. I will cast out that prince of demons by the power of the very God you blaspheme and I'll prove to this audience that there is a God. Raise this curtain right now!"

The guitarist grabbed me by the shirt. The ministers took hold of me as well. "You could be put into prison for disturbing a public meeting," one said.

"I'm prepared to go to prison for the truth and for the right to keep you deceivers from deceiving all these people," I replied.

By this time my hosts had pulled me away and were making an embarrassed effort to calm everyone down. I was removed from the building without further incident. Later, I understood that the man seated at that table who had denounced Communion was a well-known public speaker who promoted the use of LSD. Without knowing it, I had spent an evening at the epicenter of America's hippie movement and counterculture revolution.

When Discouraged— Encourage

Though God guides and performs the miraculous, there are times that everyone faces discouragement. After many weeks in New York, I became discouraged. I had no finances to return home. I missed my family. Outside the small circle of ladies I taught in the Bible study, I knew no one.

God knows we are human—He created us with emotions. He is no stranger to our struggles with discouragement. At such times, the voice of the Holy Spirit is there to encourage us, reminding us we are on a mission and we have a purpose. When God's mission and His purpose are supreme in one's heart, that's the greatest source of encouragement.

"I'm not here by myself or doing my own thing," I often reminded myself. "God has asked me to come and I'm on a mission for Him. He is going to carry me through."

One moment I would triumph over despair. The next, I would remember I had bought a one-way ticket to America. It would take hundreds of dollars to buy a ticket home. I divided in two pockets the little money I had. I kept coins in one pocket and paper money in the other.

Whenever I could get enough coins, I'd trade them for paper money and transfer the funds to my other pocket. I was desperately trying to save money for a plane ticket. I wanted to return home.

I was unable to make even one phone call to Susanne. How I longed to hear the sound of her voice. All the time we communicated through letters that seemed to crawl back and forth across the ocean. I would go to a nearby park and wander along the paths and meditate. The sunshine and the wind blowing through the trees would lift my spirit as I left the walls of the apartment behind for a few hours. I would vent my frustration, trying to find the mind of God. But I found that when we are discouraged—when we're at our lowest—God often brings us encouragement by giving us an opportunity to encourage someone else.

One day in the midst of my soul-searching, God directed my attention to a man fishing in the park's pond. I had been so discouraged that day and had been praying God would encourage me. I really didn't want to speak with anyone. As I liked fishing, I thought I'd watch him. I tried to make conversation with him, but he cursed me and I felt even more discouraged.

He didn't seem to be having any luck with his fishing, and the thought occurred to me that I could help him. I reached over and plucked his fishing pole from his grasp. He became even more agitated. Before he could retaliate I told him my God would give him a fish. He began to calm down when I launched into the story of my life.

I could see in his face that he too was battling discouragement. The minutes began to string together. Suddenly, the line jerked downward. I kept playing with the fish without reeling it in, so I could tell him all about Jesus. Eventually, a big bass flopped with exhaustion onto the river bank.

The man got excited. "That's a whopper," he shouted. "You go ahead and keep him."

"The pole is yours," I said as I handed it back to him, "so the fish is yours."

His smile widened. But I could still see the sadness in his eyes. When I shook his hand, he held my hand firmly.

"But most of all," I said, "Jesus is yours if you will only let Him into your life."

Though this was an unscheduled encounter, it was an opportunity to introduce Christ to someone who needed to hear about Him.

I continued my walk through the park, now greatly encouraged. But God was not finished. He led me to a certain neighborhood. I took a number of turns and finally came to a street where I felt God wanted me to slow down. He took me to a specific house then told me to knock on the door.

"I don't need a salesman!" a woman shouted from inside.

After several more taps at her door, she threw it open and confronted me, threatening to call the police.

"Ma'am," I said calmly, "God sent me to your door, and to your door alone, because you are planning to kill yourself with sleeping pills."

She looked at me in shock, then calmly motioned for me to enter. She told me she had three children and her husband had just walked out on her. She had no idea how she was going to care for her family on her own and she had given up in despair. I told her Jesus loved her and He had sent me to tell her He had a plan for her life. With deep sobs, she received Jesus as her Lord and Savior.

That day was a turning point for me. I still did not know how long I would remain in New York. I still had no idea when God would provide the funds for me to fly home. But God had used me to bring the light of Christ into the dark, troubled worlds of two people. And He reminded me that the darkest hours in life—the most difficult times when we are being tried and tested beyond measure—are the hours just before the dawning of His new day. We must hold on, hold fast and wait patiently before God. Then we will find that He takes care of the battle and He makes the clouds vanish.

A Salute to My Principal

One day Miss Greer paid me a visit. She knew nothing of my need. But she appeared at my door with an announcement: "Brother Colton, I want to buy you an airline ticket to anywhere in the United States you want to go."

I thanked her warmly. I decided if there was one place I wanted to go in the United States it would be to the home of my former Bible school principal, Carl Graves. He was pastoring a church in Lansing, Michigan.

Brother Graves met me at the airport and took me to his home. I was his Bible school student, and still his young kid. So, I wasn't asked to preach; instead I helped him cut his grass and paint his house. Finally, one day he invited me to hold a series of meetings in his church. I prayed, prepared, preached and God began to bless. People were healed and saved.

One night the Holy Spirit asked me to tell the congregation the story about my experience in Bible school when I wore a shirt with no back.

"Lord, how can I do that?" I prayed. "It may hurt Brother Graves' feelings. He will remember that story."

I started my sermon, entitled, "When God guides, He provides." I read from Psalm 23: "The Lord is my shepherd; I shall not want." I preached about the marvelous way the Lord guides His people and how He provides. Again, I felt the prompting of the Holy Spirit to tell my own story.

"You know," I said, "there was a young man who was marvelously saved and had a call to the ministry and he applied to a Bible college and his application was turned down three times. Why? Because he did not understand the English language."

Without naming names, I told of my journey to Bible school and the challenges I faced there. I spoke of my father's death and my financial struggles. I spoke of my ragged shirts and how I wondered if God would really provide for me. And I spoke of that fateful day when I preached in chapel and the students were offended.

I had no idea what the reaction would be. During the message, someone came from behind me and literally, in a warm hug, lifted me into the air.

"You know," Brother Graves said with a smile, "that young man was Colton. And that principal was me."

At that moment any misunderstandings between us melted away. All my past disappointments and questions disappeared. My estimation of Brother Graves, that great man of God, rose even higher. The wonderful grace of God enabled him to be so transparent with his congregation. And God honored that testimony. Across the church people broke down and wept before God and we had a tremendous altar service.

"Colton," Brother Graves said, "I'm proud of you. I'm proud that you have become the man of God I hoped you would."

"Brother Graves, I wouldn't be here without you."

We embraced—and I now understood one more reason God had brought me to America. He wanted me to salute Brother Graves, to forget the pain of the past so I could be more effective for the work of the Lord in the years to come.

A Test of Obedience

One day I was seated on my bed in the home of Brother and Sister Graves, asking the Lord to open another door for me to preach. Just then a pastor came to the front door to visit Brother Graves. From my bedroom I could hear their conversation.

"I can't get an evangelist," the minister said to Brother Graves. "My church is so small, so poor. We can't afford to get an evangelist, so we can't have revival meetings or outreach meetings." He really began to pour out his heart.

"Oh, God," I prayed, "if only I could go and preach for this man—I don't need an offering."

On cue, Brother Graves recommended me to this young preacher. "Let me introduce you to the man who can hold the meetings for you," he said. "He is truly a man of God."

Within a few days the revival meetings I had prayed for commenced.

We only had five elderly ladies and two gentlemen in the first service.

"Lord," I prayed, "how can you have a revival when you can't even have survival in a church like this?"

I spoke to the pastor after the meeting. "We must get more people," I said.

"This is a farming area," he said. "People live far

apart."

"But I see all these trucks and pickups go down this road," I noted.

"Yes, but they don't come to church. What can we do?"

I promptly asked the pastor to take a photograph of me in my national costume. We printed a flyer that said, "Come and hear what this Sri Lankan man has to say about the occult, witchcraft, demonic power and the forces of darkness. Hear what he has to say about Jesus Christ, the Holy Spirit and miracles."

I stood by the road in my costume flagging down cars. People were curious about me. When they stopped, I'd give them the information about our revival meetings.

People started to come to the meetings and God moved in a mighty way. One of the farmers said, "Brother Colton, I'm visiting from Cleveland. Our church is large and my pastor would like to have you hold a meeting for us."

"If you arrange for Sunday night," I told the man, "I will preach at your church."

At my last service at the smaller church, the pastor addressed his congregation on my behalf: "Brother Colton has not asked for money. I have not promised him even an honorarium. But I feel this man has great needs. I would like us to give him a good love offering. I want you to be a blessing to Brother Colton and his ministry."

One farmer jumped up. "I'll give $100," he said.

Another stood. "I'll give $200."

I began to think, Here is my miracle. Here comes the money for my return ticket home and to get back to Susanne and the boys.

The offering plates were full.

Thank You, Lord, I prayed, *I know my money for the whole trip is on the way.*

But when they brought me the offering, God spoke to my heart. "Son," He said, "I want you to give all the money to the pastor."

I shook my head, trying to clear my thoughts. *That cannot be God*, I decided. *If there's a man in need here, I am that man. I am the one who is halfway around the world, far away from home without a ticket to get back. Lord, this can't be You.*

Often, when it is not convenient, we refuse to listen to the voice of God. But God spoke clearly to me again: *Son, I want you to give all the money to the pastor.*

Father, I have to go to Cleveland this afternoon. If I give this money, how will I go?

Divine silence.

All right, if that's the way You want it I'll give him the whole offering.

But God wasn't finished with me. I had about $400 of my own money in my pocket before the offering.

I said all the money, the Lord commanded.

I felt so desperate. But God must be the Lord of all, and obedience must be wholehearted, I told myself. I retreated to a private room at the church.

"Oh, God," I cried out, "how can I do this?"

God reminded me of His revelation when I saw the vision of His hand in Kandy 10 years before. "Son, commitment means implicit, 100 percent obedience to the revealed will of God." I was asked to resign my church in obedience then. I was asked to give up every cent in obedience now.

I had struggled to save every dime in order to buy a ticket home. God was teaching me that He was going to lead me. And you cannot be led until you are obedient. Obedience means being willing to bend or yield—to do whatever God requires so that He can have His way. And

His way is not structured by our plans or our efforts.

Give it all, God said.

Though baffled, I was also learning total dependence on God. Our dependence is not found in the rewards we receive; our dependence is on Him exclusively.

Finally I said, "Okay, I will make that commitment, Lord." A transformation took place in my life that day. I had to come to the place I would make that implicit, total submission to the divine plan of God.

Nevertheless, sadness and disappointment filled my face. I needed God to restore my joy.

God wants us to have a song in the night. God wants us to have a song in the storm. God wants us to have a song in the fiery furnace. God wants us to have a song when everything goes wrong. And God is that song. He is the cause of the song, the theme of the song, the inspiration of the song. That's why King David sang, "The Lord is my shepherd; I shall not want" (Psalm 23:1).

God made a promise of provision so real to me that day. I realized that God was going to do things supernaturally. To do those things and to allow me to be a part of those things, God had to prepare me. He had to give me the capacity. He had to enlarge my spirit. He had to dig deep. It was painful, but I thank God to this day for that lesson.

"Pastor," I said, "I want to give you this money."

He was shocked. "What nonsense, Colton," he said. "I don't want that money. I wish we could give you even more money; you've been such a blessing."

"Thank you, but I want to give you this money."

"No, no, I'm not going to accept it."

"Listen to me. Don't argue. If you go on arguing, God will change His mind. If He changes His mind, I want you to know I'm going to take all this money back."

Suddenly that pastor hugged me. He fell on my neck and

wept like a child. "Colton," he said, "this has to be God. No one else knows my need except God. I drive a school bus five days a week to support my family. Even with driving the bus, I can't keep up with our bills. I'm in debt. This has to be the Lord."

Joy washed over my soul because God had allowed me to be part of the pastor's solution. But now I needed someone to hear from God and meet my need.

MY ADVENTURE IN FAITH

COLTON AND SUSANNE WITH SYVELLE PHILLIPS, RON PRINZING, ROY SAPP, IRENE AND CLARENCE COPE.

Principles for Living

When it comes to obeying God, there are no delays or "tomorrows." Today is the day; now is the time. This is the principle on which faith operates. If we hear God's voice, we must not harden our hearts (Hebrews 3:15). I believe when it comes to obedience, God will speak to us once or twice. After that He will give that same opportunity to someone else.

Obedience is the true evidence of our faith. When I speak of faith to people, I like to define each letter of the word F A I T H: Forsaking All, I Take Him. Commitment and faith mean complete obedience to the revealed will of God. Whatever He has revealed to us, we must be eager to do it. Don't be bothered about the things you don't know. But in the things that you know God has told you, you must obey Him at once.

Obedience often requires sacrifice. When Abraham took his son Isaac to Mount Moriah in obedience to God (Genesis 22:1-19), he journeyed three days with his son knowing he had been told to kill the boy. But in faith he understood God would somehow provide, even in the midst of sacrifice. When Isaac asked his father to identify the sacrifice, Abraham said the Lord would provide. Before that he said to his servants, "You wait here. I and the lad will go and worship the Lord and we will come back to you."

Now that is something beyond human conception or perception. God was already giving Abraham the word of knowledge he needed in order to obey. God's gifts operate powerfully when we act in faith. God sends specific words of knowledge when we are willing to make the sacrifice. In Abraham's mind he heard, *Kill the son*, because he believed God wanted him to do that. But in God's mind the sacrifice was accepted without Isaac's death because of Abraham's obedience. If Abraham had spoken from his intellect, he would have said, "I and the lad will go yonder and I will come back." But he said, "We will come back." His faith was completely alive and intertwined with his obedience.

But to arrive at that point is not easy. The human mind is always at conflict with God's heart. When I received the generous offering at that country church I could only see the money as my means of getting to Cleveland and then buying my ticket home. I wanted to hold on to what I had. After all, God had given it to me. But just as Abraham obeyed and offered back to God what God had given to him and then received a greater blessing, I was slowly beginning to realize that God had more for me. Greater victory lay ahead.

God can't give more to us when we hold onto something tightly. Sometimes we have to give up one level of blessing in order to receive the greater blessing. It was a deep step of faith when Moses chose to suffer affliction with the people of God (Hebrews 11:25). He refused the blessing of being Pharaoh's "grandson." There is a refusal and a choice of self-denial in faith that we don't pursue in our human strength and emotions. Our humanity will tell us, "I really feel that God has given this to me. I'm going to enjoy it." But as we are led faithfully by God's Spirit, we will discern those times when, to get the very best, we have to make a sacrifice.

God's Timing

The pastor of the small church drove me to the Detroit bus station. I kept trying to figure out how God was going to provide my bus ticket. I was now, again, a penniless preacher.

I presumed the pastor would buy my ticket to Cleveland. But he received an emergency phone call and, apologetically, dropped me at the curb and sped off.

I couldn't even think of a way to tactfully ask about a ticket. I stood there for a moment. "Lord," I prayed, "what am I going to do?"

Evidently, I thought, God had not impressed on the pastor the need to buy me a ticket. I decided that God's only solution now would be to send someone like a farmer who had heard me at one of the meetings to buy my ticket. I looked around the station for anyone I might know—someone God had told to follow me to the station. I walked all around the bus station. There was nobody. With nothing else to do, I sat and took my Bible and began to read it.

A bus pulled into the station with "Cleveland" across its destination sign.

"Father," I prayed, "what do I do? I don't have one cent and I have to get to Cleveland."

"Please, get your tickets," blared the announcement. Everybody stood in line to buy their tickets and started getting on the bus.

"Father," I prayed, "what am I going to do?"

I jumped into line as a way of exercising my faith. I prayed for a miracle, but people kept loading onto the bus and I was soon the fifth man from the ticket counter.

God, what am I to do? I prayed silently. *When I get to that counter, I'll have to produce the money.* I began to pray with everything in me.

When I was the third man from the counter and desperate, I tried another tactic to bolster my faith. Quickly I took my Bible and began to turn the pages as fast as I could to find a promise to hold onto. The man in front of me turned around, peered at me and my Bible.

"Hey, you're a Christian?" he asked.

"Yes," I said. "I'm a Christian minister from Sri Lanka."

He went to the ticket counter and put some cash on the counter. "Two tickets to Cleveland," he said.

Then I stepped up to the counter and asked for a ticket in faith. *Lord,* I prayed, *You'll have to put that money into my wallet.*

"Good afternoon," said the woman at the counter.

"One ticket to Cleveland," I said, pulling out my wallet. Unfortunately, it was still empty.

At that moment, the man who had just purchased two tickets turned around. "Hey," he said, "don't buy a ticket. I just bought a ticket for you. Come and sit next to me and talk to me."

Relief and gratitude rushed through me like adrenaline. I expressed my appreciation time and again to the man en route to Cleveland. I told him my story and he was greatly encouraged that God had used him.

God is never late. He is never early. He is always there on time. He never fails.

Dreams Come True

In 1967, the U.S. Assemblies of God held its 32nd General Council in Long Beach, California. To attend would be the fulfillment of a dream. But that opportunity did not come immediately.

During my travels in the Midwest, I was able to visit Springfield, Missouri, for the first time. I had always wanted to see the city that had sent Assemblies of God missionaries to my homeland. I looked forward to meeting the leaders of the Fellowship and sharing with them what God had been doing in my life and in the Assemblies of God in Sri Lanka where I was serving as Vice Chairman.

When I arrived, I discovered it was not possible to have such a meeting without an appointment. God's leading in my own life over the previous months had made written appointments almost impossible. I continued to greet each day with an invitation for the Holy Spirit to lead me. In Springfield, the Spirit again proved He is faithful—even when written appointments have not been made.

Assemblies of God World Missions kindly put me in a hotel. As I was standing in the lobby discouraged at the thought of not meeting the Fellowship leaders, I went to the check-in desk.

The young lady did not know who I was, but she

asked, "Are you saved?"

I think I must have looked like a miserable sinner at the time.

"Yes," I replied.

We had a pleasant conversation. But when I went up to my room I fell on my bed and cried out to God in disappointment.

Then the phone rang.

I picked it up and the receptionist said, "In the hotel there is another young man like you from South Korea."

"Who is he?"

"His name is Yonggi Cho. Would you like to meet him?"

"I would very much like to meet him."

Dr. David Yonggi Cho pastors the largest church in the world today. Even in 1967, Yoido Full Gospel Church ministered to several thousand people. We had never met, but he graciously agreed to join me for dinner.

"Don't worry, Colton," he said when he learned of my desire to meet with the Fellowship leaders. "I have time scheduled with them, and I'll give you some of my time."

I was ecstatic. Once again God had opened a door.

Brother Cho introduced me to the leaders. I met with Brother J. Philip Hogan, executive director of Assemblies of God World Missions. We talked about the upcoming General Council in Long Beach, California, and I spoke of my desire to attend.

"Many of our missionaries will be there," Brother Hogan said.

"I will come if I can," I said, hoping God would make a way.

With the Council just two weeks away, however, I found myself holding meetings in Cleveland, Ohio. And my pockets were empty. There appeared to be no way of attending the Council. But still I prayed for a miracle.

The pastor of the church where I was holding meetings mentioned that he and his wife were going to drive to California the following day.

Lord, I prayed, *that's what I want to do. It would be so wonderful to go to General Council and see more of America.*

After I preached that night and was headed back to my hotel, the subject came up again. "Are you going to General Council?" the pastor asked.

"Well, I am not sure yet," I said, not wanting to reveal how badly I wanted to go. "If the Lord wants me to go, I'll go."

Back at my hotel room, I began to pray, "Father, You know the desire of my heart is to go, but I have no way."

The phone rang at about 11 p.m. It was the pastor's wife. "Brother Colton," she said, "I'm not feeling too well and my husband wants to take somebody with him to the General Council. I really feel that you should go with him."

I didn't know why the Lord was bringing me to Long Beach. I only knew that I had felt an urgency to attend.

"Lord," I prayed, "You have brought me here for a purpose." I waited in faith for that purpose to be revealed.

On our way, one night in the hotel in Las Vegas, suddenly the Lord reminded me of the vision in Kandy. He told me some things I had seen in the vision in 1957 were about to be fulfilled.

Finally we arrived in Long Beach. I had never seen such a great gathering of Assemblies of God ministers. One day during General Council, Brother Hogan sought me out.

"Colton," he said, "Pastor Syvelle Phillips is here from Santa Ana First Assembly. He wants you to speak at his Sunday school adult class. Would you accept that?"

I had never heard of Syvelle Phillips but I gladly accepted the opportunity.

We drove to Santa Ana First Assembly and I taught on faith. I told the Sunday school class the story of my spiritual mother in Panama City, Florida, and how her faith made it possible for me to graduate from Bible school. She had not written to me in a long time. "She must be dead now," I said.

A man approached me after Sunday school. I realized I had seen him before; I looked at him closely trying to remember where we had met. Then it suddenly came back to me—I had seen him in the vision God gave me in Kandy in 1957. It turned out that he was Pastor Syvelle Phillips.

Pastor Phillips' face was the first face I saw in the vision. When I later shared with him about my vision, he put his arms around me and believed in me without any hesitation. Over the years, he introduced me to others I had seen in the vision, stood with me during hard times and continued to support me as he believed in the vision God gave me and wanted to see it come to fruition. Nearly a decade after the Long Beach General Council, when I was building a church to seat 1,000, it was Syvelle Phillips who stood with me in faith and prayed with me until it was accomplished. To this day, he is only a phone call away.

"Colton," Pastor Phillips said that day of our first meeting, "the woman you spoke of is not dead. She is alive. I have been in her home. In fact, her pastor is here." He introduced Pastor Gatlin from Panama City.

"You must come and meet Sister Pokorney," Pastor Gatlin told me. "Our church will fly you to Florida."

God was unfolding His plan before my eyes. At that moment, I didn't know where it would lead me—I just knew God was leading.

CHAPTER 41

Florence Pokorney and an Old Creole Lady

Sister Pokorney's home on the outskirts of Panama City was actually a small cottage. A large sign in the front yard read, "There is no water in hell." People driving down the road would get so angry at the sign they would stop and come and pound on her door. She would invite them in, and then share a tract and a simple gospel message. Many people accepted Christ.

I was told she was ailing and had been bedridden for some years. When I arrived I found her sitting on her bed cranking an old ice cream maker. She grinned and opened her arms as if to welcome me to her side. She hugged and kissed me as if I were her son.

"Son," she said as she served me a bowl of ice cream, "do you see that?"

She had pasted our family photograph at the foot of her bed.

"I knew God was going to keep me alive till this day," she said.

"How did you know that?" I asked.

"Get that little box from the shelf," she said pointing.

Inside was a stack of letters. She found a well-worn

sheet of paper, a letter I had written to her years earlier.

"Mother," I had written, "the only reward that God can give us is for me to see you one day and for me to pray for you."

"I held on to that," she said with a smile and tears. "I knew that one day God would allow me to see you."

The local newspaper in Panama City published a story of my relationship with Sister Pokorney under the headline "Miracle in Missions." It attracted quite a crowd to the church, and we had a glorious service with Sister Pokorney being brought in especially to hear me preach. Like a proud mother, her eyes never left me during the service. She was seeing the fruit of her sacrifice.

Some years later, I received word that Sister Pokorney had died. Her caregiver said that even when Sister Pokorney was semiconscious she talked about a special young man: "I know that Colton is representing God all over the world. I am so glad that I had a part in his life."

Florence Pokorney went to be with Christ after struggling for many years. But her faith had reached around the globe. God had used that faith to preserve me when I was a very young Christian. She was a rock of faith, a steadying force in my life. I know to this day that every soul I am able to touch with the gospel is one touched by the faith and sacrifice of Sister Florence Pokorney.

While I was visiting Haiti and ministering to the people there, I was reminded about a lady I had seen in my vision. I knew she had to be in Haiti. I remembered the description of the small dark lady. She had a toe missing, had a somewhat round face, kinky hair and some wrinkles on her forehead. I gave this description to the missionary and asked him if he knew a lady like this. He thought for a while and said he did not.

While we were talking about it, a young man who was a Haitian evangelist came to see him. The missionary asked him whether he knew a woman like this. He said there was a poor old lady in a village who seemed to fit my description. But he said she could not be the one, as she was illiterate. I said I would like to go and see her, if this was possible. The young evangelist was willing to take me, so we drove for some time, then we walked a long distance.

After the walk on a footpath that led to this small village with round huts and grass thatched roofs, he pointed to one of the huts. We went into a one-roomed, dark, windowless hut. I could not see anybody, but the young man began to speak in Creole. Then a short old lady came toward the entrance, and immediately I recognized her. I looked at her feet and one toe was missing. I told the evangelist this was the lady I was looking for.

The young evangelist told her in Creole that I had come from a far-off country to see her, as I had seen her in a vision in 1957. She began to reply in Creole. I understood one word, "Colton." She said, "I have prayed for him from 1957. God asked me to pray for him till I see him face to face. Praise God! My responsibility is over!" The Lord had burdened this poor lady to pray for me and my ministry, even giving my name. God moves in mysterious ways.

ROY SAPP AND COLTON AT FIRST ASSEMBLY IN
WILMINGTON, CALIFORNIA.

CHAPTER 42

Home Again

The meetings in Panama City concluded and the church flew me back to California. By now God had provided the funds through some generous believers for a return ticket to Sri Lanka. I was going to leave from California through Japan to my homeland. I even had several hundred dollars left to take back to my family.

In California I found a letter waiting from Susanne. "You sold your motorcycle," she wrote. "At least you must buy a car before you return." There was no question of the wisdom of her advice. Cars in Sri Lanka were expensive and few. Cars in America were plentiful and much less costly. But there was still a process needed to buy one. According to the law of Sri Lanka, to obtain a license to import a car, the money for it had to be deposited in foreign currency and the receipt from a bank submitted.

I looked at Susanne's letter and thought of the offerings I had been given. I knew of a car I could buy, but I was short $400. And I was leaving the United States that week.

"Lord," I prayed, "I have no more meetings and I am leaving. What am I going to do?"

The answer came in a most unusual manner.

Some Sri Lankan believers in Pasadena, California, had prepared a dinner in my honor. A friend came to pick me up. On the way to the dinner I saw several posters advertising a meeting with David Wilkerson at

Wilmington Assembly of God.

Wilkerson's book, *The Cross and the Switchblade*, had become a best seller. Teen Challenge was a rapidly growing program that was helping thousands of young people conquer their drug addictions and find Christ as their Savior.

I may never come to the States again, I thought. *Maybe I should go and hear David Wilkerson. But how could I go and hear Brother Wilkerson*, I thought, *when the Sri Lankan brothers and sisters are having a dinner for me and waiting for my arrival?*

Then I distinctly heard the voice of God: "Go to that service."

"I need to go and hear David Wilkerson," I told my friend.

"But everybody's waiting for you," he said. "You are the guest of honor. We have to go to that dinner."

He drove on.

A few minutes later I heard God speak to me again: "Go to that service."

Again I asked my friend to stop.

"You can't cancel an appointment like this," he said.

He kept driving.

A third time God made His will clear to my heart: "Go to that service."

There was no longer time for negotiation. "Turn the car around," I said. "I'm not going to the dinner. Let's find a telephone and I'll call them."

We went into a Chinese restaurant. My friend was very upset. I called the people at the dinner.

"You're late," said the lady who answered the phone. "How long will you take to arrive?"

"Something unexpected has come up," I said. "I'm unable to come."

Suddenly, instead of being the guest of honor, I was a target.

"You're too big for your own shoes now," the lady said. "You think you're too important to come to a dinner planned just for you."

Two others took the phone and tried to convince me that I should come. I wanted to melt through the floor of that restaurant. If I said God had spoken to me, they would think I was crazy. But I had to obey the Lord.

"I'll have to explain later," I said as I hung up. Turning to my friend, I said, "Drive as fast as possible to Wilmington."

When we arrived the place was jam-packed with cars.

"Please drop me at the door and find a parking space," I said. "I'll save a seat for you."

As I entered, Pastor Roy Sapp called to me, "Colton, there is no seat available. Join us on the platform. You can give the opening prayer."

I had met him just a few days earlier and had realized then that his was another face from my vision in 1957. I joined them on the platform. I prayed and sat down, anxiously awaiting David Wilkerson to enter.

The service began. Everyone was singing joyfully. But still there was no sign of David Wilkerson.

With the final solo, Pastor Sapp approached me. "Colton," he said, "David Wilkerson is not here. But God has sent you. Will you preach?"

I couldn't believe what was happening. I had thought God was giving me a chance to hear Brother Wilkerson. All along, He had planned for me to minister in Brother Wilkerson's place. Many responded to the message and I had the opportunity to pray at the altar with people who had pressing needs.

Brother Sapp called me later that night. "Colton, when

are you returning to Sri Lanka?" he asked.

"Tomorrow."

"What time is your flight?"

"Eleven o'clock."

"I want to see you."

"You will have to come early."

"Don't worry, I'll be there."

He met me the next morning and handed me a check for $500. We promptly went to the bank and deposited the money that would allow our family to become car owners again.

After several long flights, I landed in Sri Lanka. I could hardly believe God had brought me safely home. In my absence He had also taken care of my family.

A few months after I left Sri Lanka, Susanne had to move out of our home in Deanstone Place as the owner wanted it. She had no place to go. However, her brother and his wife graciously made room for her and the three boys. Very soon, she found another house. She felt it was the right place, even though it was not easily accessible and she had to depend on public transportation to send our children to school. She moved in and sent me the new address. I wrote to her that I was not sure exactly when I would return home, but indicated it would be by the end of November that year.

Some had said I would never return home; that I would never see my wife and family again. But I knew I would. I had obeyed the voice of God and He had promised to keep my family safe and in His care. Standing on Sri Lankan soil again, I was reminded that God honors His Word. If we do our part, He will do His.

CHAPTER 43

A Growing Church

Trusting God means always being ready and willing to move where He leads. After five years at the renovated horse stables, the Corea family (the owners) needed the land in order to build on the property. So in 1971 we rented a facility that had once been a nightclub.

We cleaned and painted the facility. We also performed a spiritual cleansing through lots of prayer, because we sensed there was an atmosphere of self-indulgence and decadence in the place. But when our growing congregation met for the first time in that location, the power of God fell upon us there.

As the church continued to grow, we soon realized another building would be needed. We consulted a real estate agent about finding land on which we could build a church. Because our church was only about 100 people, he took me to several small broken-down places that I realized would not offer adequate space for growth. Finally, I told him not to waste any more of my time. I needed a property suitable for a large church.

In turn, the agent wanted to find out how much money I had since I was asking for such a large property. When he discovered I didn't have much money, he determined I was out of touch with reality and decided to teach me a lesson. He said he had found the perfect location for our church. We drove to a big piece of land on which stood a three-story building.

"This is the place," he said, with a hint of sarcasm.

I walked around that land and prayed. I felt God's confirmation in my spirit. Just as the Lord had promised Abraham that the very land he walked on would become his (Genesis 13:17), I was claiming God's promise for our church. I ran up the three floors.

"This is the place. I need a price quote," I told the real estate agent.

"How much money do you have to purchase land like this?" he asked.

"Don't ask impertinent questions," I said. "That's my business. I'm going to buy this land. Get a message to the owner."

A meeting was arranged. The owner was a well-known businessman in Colombo. He had earlier leased the property to the Embassy of Israel. He asked for 350,000 rupees. I offered him 300,000. He agreed.

"When will you complete the transaction?" the owner asked.

"How long will it take your lawyers to draw up the deed?"

"Three months."

"Let's shake on it," I said, extending my hand. "My word is my bond. In three months we will purchase the property."

All those who were with me looked at me in surprise. The church treasurer reached over and nudged me under the table. He knew we didn't even have 300,000 cents in the bank.

"We don't have the money," he said later.

"Money is not the question," I said. "It's the need. We have a need and God has shown us the place suitable to meet that need."

In three months we were the owners of that property.

We began holding services in that building in February 1973. The three-story building also provided enough room for a parsonage of sorts. Our family took up residence in a few scattered rooms in the building.

In 1974 we began to hold a series of "Miracle Night" services. God powerfully blessed our congregation's faith, and many were healed of sickness and many delivered from demonic oppression. The congregation continued to grow until we were packing about 300 people into that building. By 1975, the need for a larger building was undeniable.

A number of people said we should tear down the original three-story structure and build a new facility. I had a different idea. I approached a respected elder in our church with architectural experience. "Brother Beling," I said, "I don't want to destroy the old building. I want to combine the new with the old."

He drew up the plans and amalgamated the two buildings. Now all we needed to do was collect the funds for the construction.

I saw the project to be much like the construction of the tabernacle in the wilderness and Solomon's Temple in Jerusalem. In each case, leaders asked God's people to give toward the project. I felt this building must be for the people, by the people and of the people.

I encouraged the congregation to give sacrificially in obedience to the Lord.

"Whether you give thousands of rupees or 10 rupees," I said, "it's the sacrifice given out of obedience that counts."

The people gave sacrificially. One young lady was an orphan who lived at the Salvation Army hostel. She gave her life savings—which amounted to 750 rupees.

"God understands your heart," I said. "Give a smaller

amount."

But she insisted.

There were many stories like this of sacrifice and obedience.

By the time we laid the cornerstone for the building, pledges had come in to cover the cost of the foundation. We put the record of those pledges, along with a New Testament, into the foundation. What a celebration we held that day.

"This church," I announced joyfully, "will be built because of God's faithfulness and the commitment of God's people."

In the months following, Pastors Syvelle Phillips, Roy Sapp and Ron Prinzing helped us raise more than half the funds needed for the construction of the church.

As the building was going up, one leader asked, "Colton, what are we going to put here in such a big place?"

"People," I replied.

God honored that word of faith. In January 1977, we dedicated the new church for the glory of God. It seated about 1,300 people and the building was filled to capacity.

Miracle at 3:30

One day in August 1976, a member of our church requested that I visit a young woman in the hospital who had suffered an accident and was paralyzed from the waist down. She had also lost the use of one hand. When I met Nithiya Edwards it was obvious she was very ill and discouraged. I prayed for her but we did not experience a miracle. Yet I sensed the Lord wanted me to continue praying for her, so I went back a second and third time.

One evening as we were talking, she shared with me the depth of her despair. "Pastor," she said, "don't try to encourage me. I don't believe God is going to heal me. I know my case. I know I'm going to die."

I did not accept her remarks. I interpreted them as a lack of faith. Of course, we all struggle in our faith. I had voiced to God my own discouragement on a number of occasions through the years. But I became thoroughly exasperated with Nithiya and angry at Satan that night. I left her room and went out to my car. I slammed the door, started the engine and threw it into reverse.

Why should I waste my time with a girl who does not want to hear? I thought. But as I was about to drive away, I saw the reflection of Nithiya's face very clearly in a mirror in her room. At that moment I realized that hers was another face I had seen in my vision in Kandy. I went home very thoughtful that night.

The following morning I paid her another visit.

"Nithiya," I said, "God is going to heal you."

"Pastor," she said feebly, "I told you I know the truth, and I am ready to die."

"You don't have to die," I said, "because God is going to heal you. I can't come this evening because I have an appointment with a young couple, but I will come and see you tomorrow morning." Once again I prayed with her and left.

That evening I went to visit the couple. But as I was about to tap on their door, God spoke to me clearly, "Go and see Nithiya."

"Lord," I prayed, "how can I? I'm visiting this couple for the first time at their request."

Just then the door opened. Now, if I had told them God had spoken to me just then and told me to go to the hospital, they would have thought I had lost my mind.

"I've got an emergency call to go to the hospital," I said. "I have to go."

They urged me to at least stay and have some tea.

"No, I'm sorry. I must go," I said. "I'll schedule another time for us to meet."

I drove as fast as I could to the hospital. I ran from the parking lot to visit Nithiya and saw a nurse dart into the patient's room. Nithiya had fallen from the bed and she was convulsing. I helped the nurses get her back onto the bed.

"Get the oxygen and call the doctor," I said to the nurse urgently.

"Reverend," she whispered in my ear. "She's dying."

"Lord," I suddenly prayed, faith rising in my heart, "this can't be. I have seen her in my vision."

I took Nithiya's hand and began to pray in an unknown tongue. The Holy Spirit's presence was so powerful. I think the nurses believed I was performing some kind of occult ritual.

While I was praying, Nithiya regained consciousness.

"Pastor," she said the moment she opened her eyes, "how did you come here? You said you were going somewhere else this evening."

"Nithiya," I said, "I told you, God loves you."

That night was the turning point, although doctors still claimed there was nothing more they could do for her. Her paralysis had spread; she was now paralyzed from the neck down. Nevertheless, I knew a miracle was on its way.

My ministry responsibilities were heavy as I was now the general superintendent of the Assemblies of God of Sri Lanka and senior pastor of the church. Despite our busy schedule, Susanne and I visited and prayed for Nithiya daily.

"You said You would heal her. You have to do something," I prayed. "This can't go on like this."

When I was praying God spoke to my heart, reminding me that all of this was on His divine timetable. "Son," He said, "there is a time to raise Nithiya."

I continued to pray, and then God impressed on my heart a specific date, "February 11."

I ran out of my office and drove to give the news to Nithiya.

"Nithiya," I asked, "did God speak to you?"

"Before I answer that," she said, "let me ask you a question. Did God speak to you?"

"Now, don't try to be smart. You just answer my question. Did God speak to you?"

"Yes, He said February 11."

"That confirms what God told me. Yes, February 11 is the day."

We both continued to pray over the next few days, and

God revealed to Nithiya that her healing would come at 3:30 p.m. on February 11.

I told Susanne the good news, but we didn't tell anyone else. Susanne and I asked two doctors from our congregation to come to Nithiya's room at 2:30 p.m. on February 11 for a time of prayer. We also invited her mother and my secretary to be present.

February 11 arrived. We were all praying quietly and at 3:00 p.m. I looked at my watch and said, "Let's have a Bible study." I gave them a short study about mountain-moving faith and at 3:15 p.m. I stopped the study.

"Let's pray," I said.

We all knelt around Nithiya's bed and I prayed the first prayer. After I prayed, I began to open my eyes while the others were praying. I knew the moment was near. I wanted to see what was going to take place.

At 3:22 p.m. Nithiya opened her eyes. She reported later that she saw a bright light. Her hand, which she could not use, suddenly turned and she grabbed the sheet and pulled it aside. Her legs were like sticks because they had wasted away from months of paralysis. They began to shake under the power of God. By this time, the bed was shaking and the whole room was charged with the power of God. We all began to call out to God.

Suddenly, while everybody was crying and praying, Nithiya's body began to shake and she was thrown out of the bed. She immediately knelt on the floor. The moment she knelt on the floor, I looked at my watch. It was 3:30 p.m.

I knew the miracle was complete.

"Let's stop praying and let's praise the Lord," I said.

This girl who moments before had been paralyzed stood erect. The room resounded with a chorus of praise and worship.

Nithiya walked up to each of us and hugged us. She told us about a piece of paper she had written on, days before, and given to her attendant, who was a Buddhist. It read simply, "11th February, 3:30." The attendant was now crying under God's conviction and love. She brought Nithiya's note and gave it to one of the doctors. Then her eyes flitted between the paper and a standing Nithiya.

Everyone knew God had performed a miracle. God was glorified as word of the healing spread through the church and community.

MY ADVENTURE IN FAITH

OPEN AIR HEALING SERVICES AT HAVELOCK PARK WITH
COLTON AND NITHYA EDWARDS.

Salley Zeviour

My vision in Kandy in 1957 had revealed to me faces without names. Twenty years later God spoke clearly and gave me a name without a face. He even revealed how the name was spelled.

"You will meet Salley Zeviour," He said.

God did not say where or when I would meet Salley. I just knew it would be at some point in my travels. I began to take every opportunity to seek her out.

I was in San Francisco that year with Brother David du Plessis in a charismatic conference. After Brother David introduced me as speaker, I began my remarks by telling the people I was there on a special mission.

"My mission is to meet a person called Salley Zeviour," I said. "Salley, if you are here, I am Colton Wickramaratne. Please meet me after the service."

No one did.

Having visited the United States in 1967 and having returned with Susanne for some meetings in 1971, by 1977 I had many friends there and received numerous invitations to speak.

Everywhere I went, before I preached, I would say, "I am Colton Wickramaratne. I am here to meet Salley Zeviour."

I visited many churches in the United States but I never met Salley. I decided the meeting must be intended to take place in another country, perhaps somewhere in Europe.

I was making arrangements to leave the United States for Europe when I received an unexpected call to speak for Pastor Roy Sapp at First Assembly of God in Honolulu. After preaching, I was driven to the airport for a night flight to San Francisco.

I approached the gentleman at the ticket counter. Since I was taking a 747, I asked if I could get three seats so I could push the armrests up, stretch out and get some sleep.

"Sorry, sir, we're full," he said.

"Well, will you put me in the non-smoking area?" I asked.

He gave me my boarding pass. When I boarded, I found my assigned seat. A young lady sat at the window. The middle seat was empty and mine was by the aisle. I took my seat, fastened the seat belt and said, "Did you have a good holiday in Hawaii? Did you enjoy the beaches? We have better natural beaches in Sri Lanka."

She did not respond. She seemed very agitated. I was embarrassed and pulled the magazine out of the seat pocket and began to read. As our departure time approached, the airhostess approached the young woman.

"Are you sick?" she asked.

No reply.

"Have you taken any medication?"

No reply.

The airhostess called the steward and they both tried to talk to the woman. She refused to answer and continued to appear agitated. Finally, they gathered her hand luggage and accompanied her off the plane.

Some time passed and I got the airhostess' attention. "Where is my neighbor?" I asked.

"Oh," she said, "she is too sick. We're not taking her on this flight."

I looked at the two seats beside me and a prayer of gratitude filled my heart. I had my three seats after all. I reached up to the overhead bin and took out a blanket and several pillows.

It was after 11:30 p.m. by the time we departed. Once the seat belt sign went off, I turned to lift the armrests to make my bed. The first one wouldn't budge. I twisted around in my seat to get better leverage. As I continued to tug at it I heard footsteps approaching. They stopped by my seat.

"May I sit next to you?" a woman asked.

There goes my bed again, I thought, but I turned to the woman and managed to say politely enough, "Ma'am, where is your seat?"

I was hoping she would return to her seat if I dropped a hint.

"I want to sit next to you and talk to you," she said.

I didn't want to be rude or unkind. I twisted my knees to the side so she could slip into the row. Then she did the strangest thing. She patted me on the back as she passed, as if we had been old friends.

"You are Colton, aren't you," she said in more of a statement than a question.

From the time the Lord taught me the English language in Bible school I had never run short of words. But at that moment I was tongue-tied.

"I am Colton," I said finally.

"I am Salley Zeviour. You've been looking for me on this trip."

"Yes, I was searching for you," I said, my eyes shooting wide open.

"Don't call me Salley," she continued. "Just call me sister. I'll call you brother. This is the best place for us to meet. We have more than five hours to discuss all the things the Lord wants us to talk over."

Just then the airhostess came with a snack. "I don't need anything," Salley told her. "But please give my brother a snack."

Although I had been eagerly expecting to meet Salley, I was now feeling strange all over.

"I don't need anything," I replied.

Salley said, "Then bring my brother a Coke and me a Seven Up."

The drinks arrived and Salley turned to me. "We must get down to business," she said. Then, in the face of my lingering doubts, she began to speak of things no one could possibly know.

"You have only one name on your birth certificate," she said. Even people in Sri Lanka did not know about this. I survived my birth through the prayers of my parents and when asked for a name, my mother, in gratitude to God, simply said "Samuel" for he too had been born as God's gift to his mother, Hannah.

"You have only 'Samuel' on your birth certificate," Salley said.

From there she started telling me my life story. She even mentioned why I had a limp, which stemmed from an incident as a teen. I had not even told my wife about this.

I listened in amazement. It was a night that would change my life.

Divine Roadmap

Despite Salley's supernatural insights, doubts continued to surface in my mind. *Colton, you're going out of your mind*, I thought. *You're beginning to see and hear things.*

Without any provocation, Salley slapped me lightly across the cheek. "Shame on you, brother. Right now you are thinking that you are going out of your mind."

"Yes," I said dumbfounded.

Salley continued to describe many of my life experiences. She confronted me with the resentment and bitterness I had harbored. She spoke of the deepest questions with which I had struggled.

"You are not an accident," she said. "You are a man of destiny. You have been called by divine precision, according to a divine plan and divine purpose, set in a divinely ordered manner."

I began to see new meaning in every crushing experience, every hurt, every misunderstanding I had ever endured. I began to see God's light shining on those situations and throwing them into clear relief. *Dear God*, I thought, *what confidence You have had in me, to allow me to go through those experiences.*

Salley began to explain details of my vision in 1957 and spoke of people I would later meet and tasks I was to complete. She spoke of a conference I would be organizing for ministers from around the globe, particularly from Third World nations.

"The conference will be canceled," she said.

I didn't know what to say. "Canceled?"

"But this is the way you are to approach the problem," she continued. "You are to ask to speak to the government minister who canceled all public meetings for security purposes because of the terrorist uprising."

Again, I began to doubt my senses.

"You think I'm not real," Salley said. "But you wanted God to give you my name, and He even spelled it for you." Then she spelled her name.

I still questioned whether she was real. I remembered a piece of chewing gum in my pocket. So, I offered her the stick of gum and said, "Sister, why don't you chew some gum."

Salley declined.

You can't chew gum, I thought, *as you are not real.*

Salley suddenly turned around, looked at my watch, pulled half of the gum, which was still sticking out of my mouth, and said, "You think I can't chew gum? Brother, I don't chew gum at 2:30 in the morning."

Nevertheless, she put it in her mouth and began to chew.

We continued to converse. Salley indicated that we are eleventh-hour workmen, completing the final hours of work. In Jesus' parable, she explained, workmen were sent to the vineyard in the morning, others at noon, and still others in the afternoon. In the evening when they returned, everybody received the same amount of wages. She said the Lord expected the same quality and quantity of work from those working for one hour as He expected of those who labored for the entire day. It was not the time to allow our zeal to diminish, but to allow the Spirit to guide our methods and set our priorities.

I asked about the conference again. "Please, come with me and help me implement it," I said.

"No," she said, "I was not asked to implement it, but to explain it to you."

She spoke of days to come. "The whole world will be plunged into chaos and into despair and much sorrow. Nobody is going to have the answer. The ultimate decision of the nations is in the hands of the church. The decision of the church will determine the destiny of the nations. You must expound this truth. The Holy Spirit will give you the insight you need."

The entire experience began to overwhelm me. I got very emotional. I broke down and began to cry. I felt the responsibility was too great.

She did not waver in her message in the face of my tears, but firmly encouraged me. "God has brought you through so much already," she said. "You must hold on to your joy throughout all that is ahead. God has said it; it is going to happen."

I quickly took out my handkerchief to wipe my tears.

"No," she said, "don't wipe them away. Let these tears be a remembrance to you of God's faithfulness to you up to this moment. He will continue to be faithful."

During my ministry I used to quote a promise of God in all my sermons. I would conclude my message with Christ's words: "Lo, I will be with you always, even unto the end of the age."

"You have been quoting something in your sermons," Salley said.

"Yes."

"Lo, I am with you always," she said.

"Yes," I admitted, no longer surprised by her insight.

"You have affirmed to yourself that God is a covenant-keeping God," she said. "His covenant means He is the great I Am."

I had preached that message so many times. Now I

needed to take hold of that truth and make it my very breath.

We were getting closer to San Francisco. Salley had answered all my questions. We grew silent.

"May I have your picture?" I asked suddenly.

"Just look closely at me," she said. "You will remember me."

To this day I can see her in my mind. Long, dark, flowing hair. A loosely fitting off-white garment. Olive skin. Dark, piercing eyes. If she were an ordinary person, I would have guessed her to be around 30 years. But there was nothing ordinary about her.

"May I have your address?" I asked.

"This plane goes on to San Francisco and then on to New York, but I go on," she said.

Then she began to predict what would happen when we landed. I was going to meet some pastors in San Francisco. She told me I would be on television. She said the ministers meeting me would have a problem and she gave me the answer.

We were getting ready to land.

"Promise me something," she said.

"What?"

"When you leave the plane, don't look back at me."

"I can't promise that."

"It's all that I require of you."

"All right," I conceded.

We landed. I wished her good-bye and said, "God bless you."

"May the Great I Am be with you," she replied.

The passengers disembarked. I was true to my word as I walked away from that seat. I did not look back. And I'm quite sure that an olive-skinned, dark-haired woman in a flowing robe never walked off that plane.

I was met by my host pastors in San Francisco. Just as Salley had predicted, they had a problem and to their amazement I had the answer. Later that day at the Hyatt, I bumped into a popular TV evangelist who invited me to be on his program that evening. There was no denying I had heard from a messenger of God.

MY ADVENTURE IN FAITH

AN EARLY GROUP OF TIMOTHEAN
STUDENTS.

Timothys for Today

Salley made it clear that God wanted to use my life to train and mobilize an army to serve Him. Thus, I began to look for ways to identify and prepare men and women for His service. Even as our church grew and my pastoral focus sharpened, I continued prayerfully to dedicate myself to helping others find their place of service in the Kingdom. If, as Salley said, the church was to influence the nations, then the church needed men and women who were prepared to take the gospel to every frontier.

We began the Timothean Training Program. It began with eight students at a rented house in Mattakkuliya, north of Colombo. We placed them in various roles in the church and they worked closely with us for a year. As their skills developed and we discerned areas of ministry to which they were especially suited, we sent them and others to minister in the community. If they continued to grow in their ministry, we brought them back to study further at a Bible school. Over the past 25 years, graduates from the Timothean School have launched many mission stations to further the gospel. Most of them have become pastors and evangelists; others have become committed laypeople equipped to work alongside their pastor.

Like the New Testament church we must reproduce and multiply ourselves. The Scripture says that everything was created to give birth after its own kind. For example, the apostle Paul birthed Timothy. Timothy was his spiritual son. Then Paul became a role model to Timothy. He became his older brother. Later on, he made Timothy a co-worker and gave him the responsibility of the church in Ephesus.

Most people in the East recognize the value of discipleship. When a child is intended to become a monk, at a very early age he is handed over to the chief priest of a Buddhist temple in Sri Lanka. He just follows the priest. When the priest sits and meditates, the child sits opposite him. The child observes and absorbs. It's a transferring of the guru's way of life and values into the pupil. It's an Eastern concept I wanted to reintroduce and to place within its original biblical framework. Jesus was in a Middle Eastern country. Just as the disciples lived with and followed Jesus, just as Timothy walked in Paul's footsteps and learned a life of ministry from him, so I determined these Bible students would have mentors to spend whatever time was needed with them so they could in turn take the gospel to the spiritually needy across our island and around the world.

After God implanted in me the concept of multiplication by impacting men and women through my life and ministry for Him, I thought that I could begin with Nissanka, a young man from the hills who was saved through my ministry and was serving in my home. I recognized the potential in him and knew that I should mentor him and be a role model of Christian service.

"Nissanka," I said, "if you will trust me and work with me I believe that God has wonderful things in store for you."

"What do you want me to do, Pastor Colton?"

"I would like you to be the church caretaker," I replied.

Sweep floors? Wash out lavatories? Was this the work of a minister?

But I was not assigning duties frivolously. I knew if he did the simple and humble things first, he was on the road to success.

Nissanka faithfully carried out his duties, and also was active in any area of lay ministry we assigned to him. Eventually, resources came from the church itself to send him to a Bible school. When Nissanka graduated he became one of my associate pastors. We later appointed him to oversee the ministry we had in the southern suburbs of Colombo. Through his leadership and hard work that church grew to become one of the larger churches in Sri Lanka. That church has discipled and mobilized many young men and women. Pastor Nissanka invested in them the same way we did in him.

MY
ADVENTURE
IN FAITH

AT THE CHILDCARE CENTER IN MATTAKKULIYA.

CHAPTER 48

Susanne's Burden

I have never gone a day without feeling the prayer support of my life partner. Over the years Susanne has faithfully interceded for me and faithfully worked with the pastors and members of our church to keep the ministry flowing in my absence. She also provided a loving Christian home for our children. My ministry owes much to her commitment and prayers.

Susanne shed many tears over the impoverished children of Sri Lanka, seeing them as the church of tomorrow and the future of our nation. God did a powerful work in Susanne's life and placed upon her a burden to meet the material and spiritual needs of poor and needy children. The root of that burden goes back to 1964, when Susanne was confronted by a mother with seven starving children. They hadn't had a proper meal in five days. They were now vomiting, as they had nothing but water to drink. Susanne's heart was deeply touched as she reflected on her childhood days when she lost her mother, and her father was forced to take care of his 10 children. He was able to provide only one full meal a day.

Susanne prayed, "Lord, will You give me enough so I can help people like these who are poor and needy?" She looked for something she could give and realized she had two 2-rupee notes to be used for her own children in case of an emergency.

"Lord," she said, "I have sufficient for us today; this

mother's need is greater than mine." She took the two notes and gave them to the grateful mother.

That was the beginning of a sacrificial ministry of compassion that reached out to thousands across our nation.

In 1976 a number of countries that were not aligned with one of the world's superpowers held a conference in Sri Lanka. With such a prestigious international conference attracting many heads of state, our government spared no expense in preparing for the delegates. A convention center was built. The main road from the airport into Colombo was widened.

With the restructured airport road and the landscaping on either side of that highway, a number of shanty communities had to be moved. All of those families were given government-sponsored housing, but that housing was crowded onto 17 acres in Summitpura, Mattakkuliya, an already congested part of the city of Colombo. There was no way to adequately maintain it in the years following the conference, and the area eventually gained a reputation as "hell's 17 acres." The decaying, overcrowded community became a place of poverty, drugs and prostitution. As the situation worsened, Susanne felt an ever-increasing burden for the families and children living there.

One day she was walking through those dreary housing blocks. She saw the lack of sanitation and running water. She saw children in rags playing simple games with homemade toys. She saw them smiling and laughing despite their empty stomachs.

"Colton," she said through tears, "we must do something. Not just something temporary, but something that will make a difference in these children's lives." She began to pray and seek God.

In 1978 we were able to start a childcare feeding program at the home of Pastor Elphege and Sister Ila Fernando for a few needy children. A short time later, we were able to purchase some land close to "hell's 17 acres" and establish a center.

In 1980 we were holding some meetings in the United States. One day during a long drive among some fields, Susanne looked into the sky and saw four words very clearly in the clouds: "My song of love." She glanced away and then looked again. The words were still clear. Yet, she felt she was not to say anything about it to me. She waited to discern what God was trying to tell her.

I was preaching at the church of Pastor Ron Prinzing, another dear friend whose face was one of the eight I had seen in my vision in Kandy many years before. We had a wonderful meeting and the presence of God was evident in the service. I felt impressed to give a missions altar call, and I asked Susanne to sing.

She came to the platform and sang, "I can hear my Savior calling, who will go?" When she concluded the song, someone shouted from the congregation, "Sing it again." People began to weep under a burden for the lost.

As the service concluded, a husband and wife approached Susanne. They had $2,000 they planned to give in another offering, but God spoke to their hearts that Susanne had a ministry and they were to give her the funds.

She was hesitant to accept it at first, and offered the money to Pastor Prinzing.

"Susanne," he assured, "God has a plan for this money; He intended it for you."

Then the message from the sky came back to her. She took that $2,000 and recorded an LP of her favorite songs, each becoming a "song of love" for the children she so desperately wanted to reach. She dedicated the entire proceeds from the project to the impoverished children of Summitpura. This center became a home of hope for hundreds of children who were fed daily, clothed, educated and given vocational training. Deo and Elaine Miller shared Susanne's burden and did everything possible to help her expand this ministry to the poor and needy.

The outreach started with a burden that God placed on Susanne's heart. He then provided the funding and gave her a plan to reach out to children in many parts of the country. So often people try to ignore the burdens God places on their hearts. They don't give God an opportunity to accomplish great things through them. Susanne, on the other hand, knew God wanted to reach these children. She simply made herself available to be His hand extended to children in need. As a result, many children were rescued through her obedience.

Impetus '80

In the months following my encounter with Salley, I continued to prepare for the international meeting I knew God wanted me to organize. We called the conference Impetus '80. The main purpose of the conference was to awaken the Third World church, which was like a sleeping giant.

I knew such a gathering would require careful planning, so I met with a group of consultants who had vast experience in international missions. I outlined the plan and philosophy behind the conference.

"Brother Colton," they asked, "who will lead the conference?"

It was a reasonable question. But God had told me to send out a call to ministers far and wide, especially to leaders in developing nations. Some of them were to be the speakers at the conference. The ministers who came were to be given a platform to share their God-given vision for outreach with the delegates.

"It will not have well-known conference leaders," I admitted to the consultants. "In fact, they are unknown to the present-day church at large. I was asked to make a clarion call to these leaders who are 'in exile,' who are in the wilderness, in obscurity, and who are being trained in the school of the Spirit. A gem is a gem even if it is hidden in a rubbish heap. They are being prepared and this conference is a small part of that preparation."

"What about a budget?" they asked.

"God will provide if we do it His way," I replied.

To run a conference requires a large budget. Besides, as the Lord began to impress certain ministers on my heart, I knew many of them did not have the resources to attend. So God told me to pay their way to the conference and cover all their accomodation and food expenses. There was no budget and the financial needs were enormous.

Two international Christian organizations offered to help fund the conference, but in exchange for their contributions they wanted to control the meeting. I knew God wanted me to refuse their offer and to put my trust in Him. The conference had to be run His way. Some consultants said I was planning a conference in a manner they had never seen before, so they couldn't offer much advice. But I knew I was being obedient and that was all that mattered.

Our congregation put together the logistics of the conference and we trusted God to supply the resources. Subsequently, as we prayed, funds began to pour in. We bought plane tickets and made reservations in some of the finest hotels for the pastors and church leaders who accepted our invitation.

Only five days before the conference, with Third World Christian leaders coming from some 55 countries around the world, the catastrophe predicted by Salley hit us. Many delegates were already starting their journey to Sri Lanka, when our government faced an uprising. The authorities declared a state of emergency and the president ordered all public meetings and conferences to be canceled.

Impetus '80 was to be called off.

We were feverishly working on final preparations for the conference when two police officers visited my office.

"We have to inform you that your conference has been canceled," they announced.

I remembered Salley's instructions. I called the government's junior minister and pleaded my case.

"To whom can I appeal?" I asked.

"When the president makes an order," the minister said flatly, "there is no one to appeal to. It is law; it is finished."

"Listen to me, sir," I pressed, "this is not an ordinary conference. God told me to have this conference."

I launched into my testimony, explaining how God had been leading me toward the conference since 1957. The man was dumbfounded; he must have listened to me for 45 minutes.

"God told me to do this," I said. "If you don't allow me to have this conference on this date I will go to the auditorium alone to hold the conference."

"You know we will put you in jail," the official cautioned. "We will have no choice but to take you before a judge, and I can assure you there will be a jail sentence attached."

He only fired up my faith with that threat. "Sir," I said, "when I am taken, I want you to publish what I say at my trial in our public newspapers." I was positive God would give me a message for our nation if I were thrust into such a forum.

Finally he asked me for some government references and I gave him the names of several officials I knew.

"I'll call you back in an hour," he offered with a sigh of resignation.

I didn't tell anyone in the office about our conversation. I had learned long ago that when you face a significant challenge it's better to remain silent and not infect other people with doubt. When you know God has spoken to you, you simply need to ask Him for the courage to take a stand.

For the next 30 minutes I prayed alone in my office that God would make a way.

The phone rang with the government's answer. "I've asked around concerning you," the government minister said in a tone almost friendly. "I inquired about your integrity and who you are. I give you my word; I will personally go and speak to the president. Proceed with your plans. You can have that conference."

Three years before that phone call ever coursed through those wires, on a trans-Pacific flight from Honolulu to San Francisco, Salley had said it so clearly: "Take your stand; be persuaded that God wants it done." I had. God did. And the conference moved ahead as scheduled. I also had the unique privilege of honoring my mentors Bill and Alvera Farrand at this conference.

God did everything as He said. God put Impetus '80 together. God showed me a need and gave me a plan to meet the need.

The conference was anchored on five major themes that God had given me:

1. God's method is a man and you can be that man for God.
2. Clothe Christ in the garb of the people and communicate Christ in the language of the people.
3. The decision of the church determines the destiny of the nation.
4. The power of the church is the people of the church.
5. God's Word can do what God can do.

Many of the delegates left challenged and determined to be God's person in their respective nations. Edwin

Alvarez, who at the time pastored a small church in Panama, attended Impetus '80. He returned to his nation determined to be God's man. Today he has a congregation of 10,000 and a television ministry that reaches across Latin America.

Pastor Oyakhilome, a revered elder statesman of the Nigerian church, attended the conference and left determined to be God's man for his nation. He organized Impetus-like conferences across Nigeria, which helped ignite a revival where thousands were swept into the kingdom of God.

As I watched the delegates arrive that first day and take their places in our sessions, my heart was filled with gratitude to God for His faithfulness. Many who were, at the time, ministering in obscurity would emerge as dynamic leaders. This was God's conference, not mine. God was building His church. And He used Impetus '80 to awaken the nations around the world. This conference would pave the way for Impetus '86, which took place six years later and would impact leaders from more than 80 countries.

MY ADVENTURE IN FAITH

OPENING OF IMPETUS '80 WITH GOVERNMENT MINISTERS GAMINI DISSANAYAKE AND NISSANKA WIJEYERATNE.

God's Method

One evening I appeared on a live Christian television program in the U.S.A. where the host was raising funds for a new satellite to expand the reach of his program. Without warning, he asked me to explain to the audience why this satellite was necessary for God to reach the Far East. I was unprepared for this but I gave an honest response. "This is a great television ministry, but God does not anoint television cameras or satellites. He anoints people. His Word says, 'After the Holy Spirit is upon you, you will be my witnesses, in Jerusalem, Judea, Samaria and the uttermost parts of the earth.'"

I wasn't trying to embarrass the host. I wanted the viewers to know that television is merely a tool. It is not a substitute for the work of men and women who are empowered by the Holy Spirit. God's workers are not born; they are made in the school of the Holy Spirit. And with the empowerment of the Holy Spirit, they can accomplish great things for God. Peter, for example, after he received the infilling of the Spirit, preached a message and 3,000 souls were born into the kingdom of God. The impossible becomes possible with the Spirit's empowerment.

In one small village, a girl who was illiterate was filled with the Holy Spirit. She began to pray and worship God in English, even though she did not know the language. During another service, my father was praying and

worshipping God in an unknown tongue. An educated
man walked into the meeting and stood in amazement. He
asked, "Is your father a Latin scholar?"

"No," I replied, "why do you ask?"

He said, "Your father is praying in Latin."

There is no limit to what God can do when the Holy
Spirit is working through us. God's method is a man
or woman, and you and I can be that person for God.
That is the message I communicate wherever I minister.
God's man or woman must have a vision for his or her
community, country and world. But, a vision for ministry
is not enough. We must also ask the Holy Spirit to give us
a vision of the glorified Christ. Jesus said, "When he, the
Spirit of truth, is come, he will guide you into all truth: for
he shall not speak of himself; but whatsoever he shall hear,
that shall he speak: and he will shew you things to come.
He shall glorify me: for he shall receive of mine, and shall
shew it unto you" (John 16:13,14). As our understanding
of Christ grows, our burden for the lost also grows.

Isaiah the prophet saw the calamity and chaos in Israel
when King Uzziah died. Then he lifted up his eyes and
saw the place filled with the glory of the Lord. He saw
God, high and lifted up and His train filled the temple.
His glory filled the temple (Isaiah 6:1). We also need to
see the glorified Christ with His ability and power. He
alone is able to give us the power to meet needs and rescue
people for eternity. We need the Spirit to quicken us with
the wonderful resurrection power of Jesus Christ within
us. The Holy Spirit will make us dynamic men and women
in God's service. The Holy Spirit will unfold truths to us
from God's Word—if we will simply invite Him to be our
Teacher.

We must invite the Holy Spirit to exalt Jesus through
our lives and ask Him to give us opportunities to partner

with Christ in His mission. Jesus gave the disciples the essence of that mission before He ascended into heaven. When He rose from the dead, He said to them, "Go ye into all the world, and preach the gospel to every creature" (Mark 16:15). Jesus challenged His disciples to carry on His mission and promised them the power of the Holy Spirit (Acts 1:8).

Those who partner with Christ in the mission of spreading the gospel will face opposition. But Jesus Christ has already sealed the fate of those who oppose Him. "Having disarmed the powers and authorities, he made a public spectacle of them, triumphing over them by the cross" (Colossians 2:15, NIV). He is the mighty victor over hell, death and the grave. He gives that same victory to His servants. "Behold, I give unto you power to tread on serpents and scorpions, and over all the power of the enemy: and nothing shall by any means hurt you" (Luke 10:19).

That is the revelation, the ability, and the glory of our God. It is a revelation that everyone needs to know. That is why Jesus said, "I will build my church; and the gates of hell shall not prevail against it" (Matthew 16:18). There is no strategy, there is no power in hell to ever withstand, defeat or overcome the church of Jesus Christ.

The church of Jesus Christ is not a denomination. The church of Jesus Christ is not an edifice. The church of Jesus Christ is not a constitution or a set of theological beliefs. The church of Jesus Christ is the people of the church. God's method is every man, woman and young person who makes up His precious Body, the Church, on this earth.

We need that revelation. As much as we need a revelation of the hopelessness of the world, we need a revelation of the ability of God. This type of vision, when received, changes us. We begin to lose ourselves. We begin to see the inadequacy of humanity and the unmatched power of God. When we comprehend His greatness, we also understand our purpose. We belong to a royal priesthood. We are a chosen generation. Each person is a chosen vessel, separated for the Master's use. Therefore, we can move wherever God leads us with an assurance that He is helping us accomplish His purpose. And because we are His, He gives us understanding of His heart and power.

When we begin to visualize who we are in God, we begin to grasp the full meaning of Philippians 4:13: "I can do all things through Christ which strengtheneth me." When we are in Christ, we become an outlet of God's power and authority.

You need to be God's person, in God's place, in God's time, doing God's will.

The Unknown Things are Known to Him

The faithfulness of God is such that He remembers your needs—when you have not even asked Him to meet them. The eyes of the Lord are upon His children, and He knows their needs before they ask Him. We wish to recall one of those special events in our lives.

Susanne and I never considered buying a house or a block of land, as we never thought of owning a house. We were quite content living in rented houses for about 25 years, moving from place to place. For some years we were able to have our worship services in our home while making use of the bedrooms for ourselves. The church was now built to seat over 1,000 people.

At this time we were compelled to move farther from the church, as we could not afford the rents in the city. This was becoming a problem, so we decided to visit our former landlord and asked him if he would sell a small plot of his land to us. He said that it was not possible but that his brother had some land that he wanted to sell, and he wanted us to meet him. When we visited his brother he gave us the details of the land and requested us to have a look at it. When we visited the land we found that most of it was marshy land. We, however, felt that we had set our foot on the right place and that this was what the Lord wanted us to get. We then decided to work on it.

We knew that a few pastors who were very interested in our ministry had put aside some money for us. They said, "When you buy a home for yourselves we will give the money to you," as even some gifts given to us personally were used for the building of the church. We remembered this promise, and felt that this could be the starting point.

The owner of the land, who was a Buddhist, seemed very keen to sell it to us. When the final transactions were made, he said to us, "I am not a greedy man. I know if I keep this land a little longer I can make a lot of money. But Reverend, I am so happy to sell this to you."

When we look back we realize that his words were true because the property now, after approximately 20 years, is very valuable.

This was indeed the Lord's work and we accepted this as from His hand. Even though we were not interested in building a house for ourselves, the Lord opened a door for us and gave us this three-fourths of an acre of land. Today, each of my sons own a block on this land and has a home of his own. My daughter too owns a piece of land in the neighborhood.

This was far beyond our expectations. When you put God and His kingdom first He certainly takes care of all your needs.

His plans, though hidden to us, will be revealed at the right time—His provision never fails!

A Consuming Vision

When I pastored the congregation in Kandy, I often fell at the altar of our small church and prayed for hours for lost people. When we comprehend the consequences of their unbelief, the mission of reaching them becomes a greater priority in our lives. We cannot live in the same manner as before. The Great Commission—taking the gospel to people walking toward destruction—begins to monopolize our thoughts and prayers. In Kandy I lost my appetite because the mission became more important than food. People used to look strangely at me because I cried in anguish over those who did not know of Christ's atoning work. How could people have a social relationship with me when they couldn't communicate with me through my tears? My ability to sleep also vanished. Reaching the lost took precedence and, night after night, I would sit on my bed and cry over souls.

Where there is no vision, people will surely perish (Proverbs 29:18). A vision of the lost is not something a theological college gives us. It is not something we acquire from a book. It is not something we receive by listening to a preacher. This is something the Holy Spirit must give us. And He will give it to us when we reach out beyond our church doors determined, under the power of the Holy Spirit, to reach people for Christ. A true vision of the lost will melt our hearts and we will cry out, "My God, I can't do this without Your help." Reaching those who need to experience the saving grace of Christ becomes more than life to us, as we recognize our complete insufficiency and reliance on Him.

Every person in the Bible was as human as we are, but these men and women of God changed the destiny of their generations. We too are called to change the destiny of our generation—not just to play church. We are men and women with a mission and we must fulfill it. That is why we need His vision. We need to position our hearts so God can captivate our eyes and ears by His Spirit and reveal His vision for a lost world and His purpose for our lives.

Whenever I look back, I stand amazed at God's faithfulness, for none of His promises have failed. A highlight in the vision God gave me was the building of the church complex in Narahenpita (Colombo 5.) The faith edifice located in Kollupitiya (Colombo 3) became totally inadequate and I needed to take a giant step of faith once again. To fully implement the vision God gave me, we needed to build a church that would seat at least 5,000 people, with added facilities for teaching, training and other programs.

I needed a fresh supply of God's grace and wisdom for this step of faith. Some of the leaders working with me felt the new building project could not be accomplished and strongly advised me against pursuing it. But I knew without a doubt our God is a great God who provides all the resources we need to achieve what He commissions us to do.

As our leadership reached a consensus in faith, we committed to purchase a block of government-owned land that had come up for sale, a little over 2 acres. The availability of such a large plot in the heart of Colombo was in itself a miracle. Our people met the challenge and gave sacrificially, and God honored their faith and their giving and opened the windows of heaven in blessing.

But it was a long journey, and I battled my own doubts despite God's leading.

"Lord," I prayed, "is this building of such tremendous cost really Your plan? Give me a sign of confirmation." I felt like Gideon with his fleece.

A few days later, a lady walked into my office and placed 1.2 million Rupees on my desk for the building. This was a massive and sacrificial sum for one person to give. But this was the sign of confirmation in answer to my prayer.

We held a special service to invite our people to give toward the ongoing construction. We invited Pastor Rick Seaward of Singapore, a man of faith and a missionary statesman, to be our guest speaker. He encouraged and challenged the people to give in faith and sacrificially. He said God had spoken to him during his flight to Colombo and told him that for every Rupee the people put in sacrificially, his church in Singapore must match it with another Rupee. When we received the offering that Sunday it was a financial miracle never seen before in the Sri Lankan church.

We purchased the land in 1991 and God enabled us to dedicate the building in November 1999. Our people continued to give faithfully and sacrificially, not only of their finances but of their time and in volunteer labor as well. It was amazing to watch the facility take shape, a task so many thought was impossible.

During construction God gave me an unusual confirmation I was moving in His will. An Indian engineer working in the Middle East was assigned to come to Colombo to recruit staff. He had declined in view of unstable conditions in the country. He shared his concerns with his prayer group, and received specific direction that he should come to Sri Lanka and contact a person named Colton. Through a series of clearly miraculous events, he finally met me. The stranger spoke of his own work for God. He mentioned two instances of how he had implemented something God had shown him, a confirmation of something God had shown me too.

When I began to speak of my own church building plans the man interrupted me.

"In 1989, God gave me a vision," he said. "I saw a large building lifted from the ground and I counted 72 pillars. Under the building there were parked cars. Cars were driving up to the first-floor level, which had four doors. Thousands of people were coming and going. They were not Westerners or Chinese; they were Asians. I could not figure out where this building was."

This was clearly our building. There were to be 72 pillars visible in the construction. Two years before our plans were even thought of, God had revealed them to this man in precise detail.

The People's Church today ministers to more than 7,000 weekly, touching all levels of society in our city. Its missions program reaches to other parts of the country and overseas as well. God told me this church would be the busiest place in the city. I can see that promise being fulfilled before my eyes.

The vision God gave me was all about people. The Holy Spirit affirmed to me God's love for the world. God is not willing that any should perish. The gospel of the Kingdom must be preached to all nations. The Lord's command is to go into all the world, to preach, teach and make disciples of all nations. In God's plan, every believer is included in this Great Commission. No one is excluded. Only you can exclude yourself. God has invested the riches of His grace in the gifts and ministries of His people.

MY ADVENTURE IN FAITH

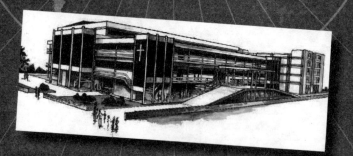

THE NEW CHURCH BUILDING AT NARATTENPITA.

CHAPTER 53

Implementing a Vision

Through the years I have told many people about the vision for ministry God has given me. In response, some have said, "That is impossible—unrealistic." I have heard such comments more times than I care to remember. As much as I wanted to write off such people as foolish, I had to remind myself they were not wrong. Based on the common-sense laws of life, they may have been right— because they could not see what I saw through the Spirit. Therefore, nothing is to be gained by ridiculing these cynics as blind, deaf or faithless. We may simply have a vision they do not have. But when a vision is implemented, people will begin to see it. They will begin to realize God is at work. To wait for everyone to see the vision can deal a fatal blow to its implementation because some people have to see it to believe it.

Implementing one's vision is not easy. But if God has spoken, we must be determined and not listen to the doubts of others. We must have courage. We might not be able to convince every person at the start, but we must put our hands to the plow and not look back. We must keep plowing. We can never give up.

When we start implementing a vision for furthering God's kingdom the process requires that we convey and impart vision to others. As we do that, the vision comes into focus and new details present themselves. New goals become clear. But sometimes the vision God gives us fades away because we assume the first phase of a revelation or vision is all that God had in mind. As a result the vision remains narrow and never expands. But visions are often revealed to us in phases. Daily we must seek direction from God, asking Him to further reveal His plan to us. He works this way because He understands us. He knows if we saw the complete vision, we would perhaps shudder with fear and never attempt the enormous tasks He's calling us to perform.

When we earnestly desire a vision from God, we live with a sense of expectancy. Each day we look for new steps that can be taken that will lead us further on in the journey towards fulfilling it.

I don't talk as if I'm one who received God's leading and acted on it perfectly and immediately. There were aspects of the vision that I put off. It was so difficult for me, after waiting so many years, to get started on Impetus '80 and to step out and do it. It was almost an impossible task. But God is faithful. As I took small steps, I began to see more and more of what God wanted me to do. As the details of the vision unfolded, every step led to another step—the vision began to grow in me.

Brokenness and vision often go hand-in-hand. Brokenness occurs when we recognize our complete reliance on God and our desperate need for the Spirit's power. We put our trust in the power of God and realize that, despite our weaknesses, we stand in Him complete. We stand in the strength, in the power, in the might of the Holy Spirit and we begin to draw upon God's unlimited resources. This understanding naturally results in greater vision.

Identifying with the needs of people is another

prerequisite for vision. At one stage in my life, I didn't realize I had become selfish. My needs came first. But one day my eyes were opened. I realized I was playing church, oblivious to the spiritual needs of others. It was then— when I identified with the needs of people and Christ's love for them—that I received a vision for ministry that changed my life. This led me out of selfishness into selflessness, from receiving to giving, from my comfort zone to reliance on the Spirit. I moved from the natural to supernatural. And I also discovered that the afflictions we go through to receive and implement a vision do not compare with the abundant blessings that await us if we follow the leading of the Spirit.

MY ADVENTURE IN FAITH

COLTON AND SUSANNE.

Precious Time

If we waste time, we will never recapture it. The Bible exhorts us to "redeem the time, because the days are evil." But time well spent will pay eternal dividends. As a young minister, the Lord showed me I had to rearrange my life and exercise self-discipline if I was going to be the man God wanted me to be. I had to move quickly to make lifestyle changes. This rearrangement of my priorities enabled me to fulfill the vision God had given me.

Sometimes a vision God gives us may never become a reality—or may not happen in a timeframe we understand. That is the mystery of God's sovereignty and the way His will interacts with ours. God can entrust us with a vision, but our will must submit to His will in order to bring the vision to fruition in His time. There are certain things I expect to see in the days to come. I believe they are going to work out to the extent that I am obedient—and others are obedient—to the voice of the Lord. But I also know these things may not come to fruition because they involve other people, and I cannot control what they do. We must accept the fact that God is going to fulfill His plan in His way, in His time. If a vision is of God, it will work and it will continue working.

God desires to work through men and women. In 1957 when I received the vision, God told me that when there were "responsible people to bear responsibility" not only would I be able to entrust the ministries of my church to them, but more importantly that would be a prerequisite for the end-time revival when God would pour out His Spirit on all flesh. Over the years I have repeatedly emphasized this truth. He desires to entrust the burdens of His heart to another heart with which He is in communion. God is "not willing that any should perish, but that all should come to repentance" (2 Peter 3:9). That is His burden. God wants us to share His burden and His sense of urgency. He wants us to work on that burden by fulfilling the command that Jesus gave us: "Go ye into all the world, and preach the gospel to every creature" (Mark 16:15). He wants us to make disciples, to build the kingdom of God. That requires us to carry out the plan that God has in mind for us, for our community, for our country, for our world.

We cannot rely on old strategies and use antiquated tools and expect a harvest or a great revival. But if we are operating according to God's vision it will change our pattern of thinking. It will bring fresh thoughts into being. It will make us more creative. As we put God and His vision first, we will have right values and we will put everything else in its proper place.

Once God gives us a vision, we cannot waste precious time. We must learn to use time profitably and dedicate the major part of our time to the work of God and to building His kingdom.

A man or a woman is needed who will say, "Lord, I need Your vision. Open my eyes that I may see. Lord, quicken my spirit that I may be what You want me to be." God has given each man and woman great potential and unlimited possibilities. We are God's ideal method. We are God's plan. We are God's way. We are the ones whom God wants to use. The Lord has specifically shown me that He wants to use each of us—no one is to be excluded.

All who are willing will be included. Without reservation, we need to say, "Lord, take me and use me. I want to be that vessel, that woman, that man You have been seeking. I am available now."

God wants men and women He can call on in every country, every community and every local church. Every local church is a segment of the universal body of Christ. According to the Bible, the Church is His bride. And the Holy Spirit is working sovereignly to purify and prepare every believer within the Church. The Bridegroom, Jesus Christ, is at the door. He is coming back to earth.

In 1977 when I met Salley, she explained to me that Jesus was ready to return to earth, that He was already standing up ready to come but the Father was restraining Him as the Church was not ready. He is not coming to receive unto himself a harlot or an impure bride. She explained to me that He is not only coming for a Church that is without spot or blemish, but for a radiant, dynamically active and growing Church. Her adornment as the bride of Christ was to be with ornaments such as the fruit of the Holy Spirit and the vibrant operation of the gifts of the Holy Spirit.

Each person needs to take time to seek the Lord with all his (or her) heart. Say, "Lord, I recognize after reading Brother Colton's testimony that I need a vision. If he can be your man, I too can be a person for God. I want to be used of God. Lord, take me, use me, make me to be a person for You and Your kingdom. I am available. I want to give of myself completely."

If you will do that, God can use you. The church needs you. Your responsibility is great and your work cannot be done by human wisdom, natural resources or human ability alone. It is "not by might, nor by power, but by my spirit, saith the Lord of hosts" (Zechariah 4:6).

Therefore, I urge you in the name of the Lord Jesus not to waste time. Seek the Lord and call upon Him. "Seek the Lord while He may be found. Call upon Him while He is near." Let Him not pass you by. The day of opportunity is almost coming to a close, but you can still be that 11th-hour workman, doing the crucial work of this hour.

Will you accept the challenge? Will you say, "I am available for whatever task or vision You give me"?

Susanne's Illness and Recovery

Life's challenges never cease. Even as Susanne and I watch God bring about the vision He gave me and see His church move forward in Sri Lanka, we encounter circumstances that bring us back to the foot of the Cross in utter dependence.

It was one of the most devastating experiences of our lives when we learned in July 1996 that Susanne's kidneys were badly damaged. The diagnosis was irreversible end-stage renal disease. For Susanne there was no panic, no tears, no questions such as "why me?" She accepted this trial with the calm assurance God was in control. Even as the disease progressed, Susanne would say with St. Paul, "For me to live is Christ, and to die is gain" (Philippians 1:21).

Let me share some of Susanne's own vibrant testimony:

When the doctors informed me my kidneys were affected, I felt as if a dark cloud came over me. It was not the prospect of going through this illness and perhaps succumbing to it. I was overtaken with grief at the burden this would place on my husband, our children and their families.

We had no medical insurance. A short time earlier, when my brother Elphege was diagnosed with renal failure, I witnessed his family grapple with the stress of caring for him and the stupendous financial burden.

That first night at the hospital, I struggled with my thoughts. "Lord," I prayed, "if it is Your will to take me, I shall be happy to be with You. But I cannot bear to see my family go through this traumatic experience. Give me peace to know You are in control and You will take charge no matter what the cost or circumstances may be. I need a deep assurance You are holding my hand and You are taking me through."

I pleaded with the Lord for perfect peace that night. Alone on my hospital bed, while voicing my thoughts to the Lord, I fell asleep.

The next morning I was amazed at the deep peace that flooded my heart. I felt a calmness and a complete release from the burden of the previous night. That peace carried and sustained me during six years of sickness and nursing, waiting for a kidney transplant that did not seem to be possible.

Susanne's dialysis required four hours a day three times a week. She was often nauseous and at times experienced unbearable itching. Besides her strict diet, the greater challenge was the restricted fluid intake.

Much prayer went up on her behalf. We did not falter or doubt God's great love for us and His infinite wisdom in all our affairs. God is our Healer. He has provided not only the healing of our souls but also the healing of our bodies through the atoning work of Christ. It is also true as we go through life our bodies go through wear and tear. Our redemption will only be complete in eternity when this corruptible body will put on incorruption.

We continued to follow the doctor's advice and did all we could to care for Susanne. She made several visits to India and even to Dallas, Texas, in the U.S.A., each time taking a volunteer kidney donor with her. Tests showed her immune system would reject a new kidney. After a final unsuccessful treatment at Apollo Hospital in New Delhi, Susanne determined to give up the idea of a transplant.

One day, as she was on the dialysis machine at the Sri Jayawardenepura General Hospital, she collapsed unconscious. She was rushed to the Intensive Care Unit. I stood outside praying. After I had been waiting for a long time the doctor walked up to me.

"Reverend," he said, "we have done everything possible for your wife, but she is unconscious and is on a ventilator." He then asked me if I had any questions.

"Doctor," I said, "there is nothing more to ask since you have done your best."

My children and I visited Susanne daily as she lay unconscious for 14 days. I prayed fervently. The church called for a special prayer meeting to intercede for her recovery. Many people came to pray for Susanne the whole night through.

A young man approached me at that meeting.

"Pastor Colton," he said, "we know you are a fighter. When your mother died you would not let her go, but brought her back to life by calling on the power of God. The day your mother knew it was her time to leave the earth, she asked you to stay away from her, as you would try to keep her back the same way you are now trying to keep Sister Susanne back. I think you should release Sister Susanne so the Lord can take her home."

I went home and knelt by my bed. I was a broken man. "Lord," I prayed, "Susanne and I have been together for many years. I release her into Your hands, though it is a very hard thing for me to do. You can take her unto yourself."

I got into bed and fell asleep. It must have been past midnight when I was awakened by a voice. Fully awake, I realized the Lord was speaking to me.

"Who are you to grant Me permission to take Susanne? I do not need your permission to take her. I can take her, I can take you and I can take your youngest granddaughter, Dilani. Remember, you are only a gardener. I am the Owner of the entire garden. You have no right to walk into My sovereignty and to tell Me what I should do. I have told you you should obey Me and do My revealed will. You have told your congregation you will always obey My revealed will. I have told you to pray for the sick and carry out my commission. Just obey Me. Do not try to take my place."

Immediately I told the Lord I was sorry and that I would unquestioningly obey His revealed will.

The following morning, I went to the hospital. Susanne was lying there like a corpse. I began to fervently pray. I asked the Lord to restore her to health. There was no answer. I prayed again in the afternoon and evening, but Susanne showed no sign of movement.

I went home and went to bed, this time thanking the Lord that He is the Healer. The following day as I went early in the morning and entered the Intensive Care Unit, a nurse stopped me.

"Please do not go in," she said.

The curtains of Susanne's cubicle were drawn. I thought the end had come. In spite of the nurse, I walked to the cubicle. As I drew the curtains aside, to my utter surprise I heard my wife say, "Nurse, let him come in. That's my husband."

God restored Susanne to life!

Susanne has this to say:

During the two weeks I was unconscious I had an unusual experience. I saw a huge tree behind a big gate. I was inside and could not come out. I could see my husband and children running to and fro trying to get me out.

Many people say, when they had experiences like this, they would see heaven open and they would see the Lord. My experience was different. All I can think is that my life was almost over, but the prayers of my family and God's people brought me back to serve Him which I continue to do with all that is within me.

God brought Susanne back to life.

This story would not be complete without Susanne's eventual transplant, which has held good up to the time of this writing. After her initial recovery, she had gone on a better though more expensive form of dialysis that she found more tolerable. Due to the situation in the country at the time, there was a problem with the availability of the bicarb dialysis.

Again, let Susanne share her thoughts:

I wanted this type of dialysis so I could feel a little better, but I did not share this with anyone. Colton was leaving for meetings in the States and asked if I would like to accompany him. At first, I refused. I did not want him to have to care for me, which would hinder his ministry. But he asked me again, and I decided I should go so I could have a change of dialysis. I planned to stay with a friend.

I did well on the trip until we reached California. The very next day, I developed chest pains. Our dear friend Pastor Ron Prinzing drove me to a hospital where a friend of Dishan's was working. On my arrival she was able to assist me. After being dialyzed and treated for five days, I felt better and asked if I could leave. The doctor there asked me where I was going for my next dialysis. When I said I had just arrived and had not made any arrangements he explained he could not release me until he knew where I was going for my next dialysis.

Unknown to us, God was at work. This was His provision. From that point, the door opened for dialysis three times a week at no charge. Transport to and from the hospital was provided, again free of charge. God wonderfully provided through friends a lovely apartment at Long Beach, a vehicle at our disposal and everything we had need of for over a year.

I developed a more severe heart condition and was admitted to St. Mary's Medical Center in Long Beach for an angioplasty. The nephrologist visited me, examined the reports and declared I could go through with a kidney transplant. My antibody level was finally in the correct range. My hopes rose.

Colton's cousin, Siyanthi, had been waiting to donate a kidney and was disappointed when earlier attempts failed. She flew to California. We went through the transplant at Harbor UCLA Hospital and I was supposed to leave by the fifth day after the operation.

It was not to be.

On the fifth day the doctor told us there was a rejection. I was back on dialysis and then on plasmapheresis— on a machine for six hours at a time. But I was not dismayed—I knew the Lord knew everything that was happening. Praise God! The transplant finally turned out successful.

The Lord does all things well. During my transplant operation and subsequent recuperation—a month long stay at Harbor UCLA Hospital—I was treated with much *kindness and loving care by the doctors and nurses. As I was leaving, they gave me a bill stating the cost of my operation as well as that of the donor, the nursing care and everything else during my lengthy hospitalization. It was $0.00.*

I had no words to express my gratitude to the Lord and to all the dear ones who helped me and made this possible. The peace the Lord said He would give me throughout my illness and that He so implanted in me stayed with me through those years of trial and testing. There was no burden to my family or the church, except for the dependence on them for their love, their caring and concern knitted together with their prayers. I am so thankful I am able to be at my husband's side and help my children as together we joyfully serve Him, our incomparable Savior and Lord.

God will perfect that which concerns each and every one of us if we have the courage to trust Him and commit all our ways and all our days to Him. God's work must be done and His kingdom extended while it is day and before the night comes. We can give or take no rest till we cast up the highway that brings us back the King!

EPILOGUE

After the Storm

The church that began in my home has grown to become one of the largest churches in the nation. People's Church attracts thousands of people from across Colombo every week. My youngest son, Dishan, now pastors the church. As revealed to me in my vision, this church will continue to impact the nations.

When the tsunami struck Sri Lanka in December 2004, Dishan called the church to action, and that very day it became the busiest place in the city as people worked day and night to help victims of the disaster.

Thousands also gathered at our church to pray for the victims and for our nation in this time of distress. When I stood to address the congregation, I reminded them that we serve a God who can be called upon in the midst of the greatest storm. "The God who calmed the Sea of Galilee is the same God who calms the troubled heart in every storm of life," I said.

In the months following, I saw our churches mobilized as never before to share Christ's love with families who had lost all hope. Our churches came to the rescue of thousands of men, women and children, providing them with food and shelter. The reality of the phrase God gave me years ago—"The power of the church is the people of the church"—was never more evident.

So, in the wake of this great tragedy that crashed upon us from the ocean's depths, I see new beginnings. I see

God birthing new vision and raising up people to serve Him. I see the same God—who from the creation of this world has been drawing people to Himself—using even the most devastating circumstances to show them His love.

I have many more miles to go. The Lord has not finished with me.

"Lord," my son Eran prayed at my bedside when I had a medical emergency recently, "he has not finished what You have asked him to do. Please raise him up."

God gave me new strength that day, as He so often has over the years. I know He will enable me to accomplish all that He has laid upon my heart to do. He is the same great I AM today as He was in eternity past and as He has been with Susanne and me all along our journey in faith.

The church God used us to plant and establish is going from strength to strength. Dishan has taken on the responsibility of leading the church along with our other two sons, Chrysantha and Eran, and an ever-increasing team of dynamic leaders. I can see many things the Lord showed me yet unfolding before me. I know He will give me the grace and strength to be faithful till my work is done. What a wonderful God we serve!

To contact Colton or Dishan Wickramaratne,
write to:

160/30 Kirimandala Mawatha
Colombo 5
Sri Lanka
colton@peopleschurchsl.org
dishan@peopleschurchsl.org

For a complete list of books offered by
Onward Books, Inc., please call or write:

Onward Books, Inc.
4848 S. Landon Court
Springfield, MO 65810
417-890-7465

Or visit our
Web site at: www:onwardbooks.com